Foreword

You might say "what?" And even be somewhat offended by the title. What could be light about the tragedies and horrors suffered by so many during the course of the war in Vietnam? Well, we all know that sometimes laughter and banter between soldiers helps them cope with the unthinkable, but in the context of this book the word lighter has a different meaning. It describes a vessel that transports cargo from a large ship to a smaller one that can come to shore where no docking is possible for large ships. The operational process for such an undertaking is called lightering, lighterage, or LOTS, (Lighterage Over the Shore).

My training in the US Army ultimately led up to being involved in lightering at Cam Ranh Bay, Vietnam in the South China Sea and then at Sattahip Thailand in the Gulf of Siam while being assigned to the 165th Transportation Company, Lighter Amphibious.

Author's Note

This book is a memoir. It chronicles people, events and places in as true an account that memory alone, without research can provide.

Names have been altered to protect the privacy of the individuals contained herein.

Chapter 1

As a child I remember always being fascinated by the regalia and all things military. My father and mother met in Faverney, France during World War II. They ultimately married in March 1945, in a French village named Rambervillers. When the war ended my father chose to stay overseas since he had his wife with him, and he worked for the US Army. During the war he had served with the 649th Engineer Battalion, creating maps from aerial photographs. Since he had experience with photography and the reproduction processes like Photostats he was hired to microfilm German war production plans to be studied by the U.S.

When my mother became pregnant with me, my father sent us to his family in the Bronx, New York. He wanted me to be born in the United States, and after an ocean liner voyage for my mother I was born in Manhattan at New York Hospital.

When I was two years old we returned to Europe and lived in Frankfurt, Germany until my mother and I left due to the tensions between the Allies and the Soviets during the Berlin Airlift. We again lived with my grandmother and grandfather at the same address as we had earlier. My father stayed in Germany for something like two years more before finally joining us. Among my dad's souvenirs was a German officer's hat. I loved to play with the hat and would proudly say that I was a "Rutenant." My mother would often correct me and tell me that the correct word was Lieutenant. I would not have any of that so "Rutenant" I remained.

My mother and I had occasion to travel by train to meet my father who was looking into an employment opportunity in Philadelphia, Pennsylvania. My mother was to see if she liked the neighborhood we would be in and also the city itself. I was four years old, it was 1950, and World War II was still very much on people's mind, especially with the Korean war starting up.

Sitting across from us on the train, in the type of seats where we were face to face with other passengers, sat a US Army soldier. This, of course, caught my attention being accustomed to soldiers, so I immediately struck up a conversation with him. I told him very proudly that my father was a "Rutenant in the German Army." My French war bride mother nearly fainted. She explained to the soldier in her French accent that her husband, "Was in fact in the US Army and that I was confused due to the souvenir hat being German." My mother went on to tell the soldier all about my father's service in the 649th Army Engineers and all the campaigns in which he took part. She did this in an effort to convince the GI that my dad had indeed been in the *US Army*. As many times as that story was told we never really knew if that soldier had been truly convinced.

In sixth grade, at PS 47 in the Bronx, one of my classmates, Frank Rinaldo, came to school wearing a Navy uniform, complete with a white web belt and white leggings. I was immediately intrigued. I questioned him about the uniform and he told me he belonged to an organization called the American Bluejackets. It was a naval cadet organization that met every Friday night at PS 36 on Castle Hill Avenue in the Bronx. There were five stations making up the American Bluejackets in New York City. We were known as Parkchester and other stations that I can remember were, New Dorp and New Utrecht. I can't recall the other two.

My friend Emanuel Giambolvo and I went to PS 36 on a Friday night to join. We were told to come back next year. What? As it happens there were no meetings held during the summer months because the school was closed. Well, we waited out the summer and returned early the next school year to enlist. I can remember one Friday night when my father drove us to the meeting in his 1951 Pontiac and we heard on the car radio that the Russians had launched a satellite named Sputnik. This would have been October 4, 1957. My father seemed upset by this news saying, "How the hell did the Russians do that when our stuff just blows up?" But concern for that news was lost on our young minds and our naïveté.

Our first assignment in the Bluejackets was the recruit platoon. This is where we learned marching, close order drill and the manual of arms. The rifles we used were 1903 Springfield bolt action weapons that were made safe and inoperable, or mock rifles known as cadet trainers.

Either way you could still operate the bolt which was necessary to execute the command, "inspection arms," and also to rotate the rifle by pulling the bolt back and spinning the rifle simultaneously for a trick drill maneuver.

While in the recruit platoon we wore only the Navy work uniform of a light blue chambray shirt and bell bottomed dungarees. You were not allowed to wear the dress blues until you successfully passed the training phase and were assigned to one of the three platoons. There was an A, B and C platoon. "A" platoon was considered the best and, as such had first pick of the recruits. I was selected for "A" platoon, a proud moment in my eleven-year-old life.

There was an initiation held once a year. I later learned it was patterned after the U.S. Navy's King Neptune initiation held for those sailors who were for the first time crossing the equator. This initiation had a reputation for being very scary. Rumors told of horrible things happening to you. You could evade the torture by just not showing up the night of the initiation. Since there was no makeup date for those who missed it you needn't worry until the next year.

I usually came to the dinner table in my uniform ready for my father to drive me to the meeting immediately following. On this night I did not have my uniform on because I decided not to go to the meeting and thus avoid the initiation. My father asked, "Why aren't you in uniform?" I told him about the initiation. He looked at me and said, "Get your uniform on, you're going tonight. If you signed up to be a sailor or soldier you can't shirk your duty or avoid the unpleasant aspects." A lesson learned.

As it turned out, and as my father probably surmised, we had a lot of fun. The "horrible" things that happened to us were being blindfolded and placed on a wooden board picked up off of the deck just a few inches, but the conversation being held by the people lifting the board was, "That's it, get it higher and place it on your shoulder." Then you were pushed or spilled off just to learn you were an inch off the deck. They took the precaution of having spotters stand by to assist you if you lost your balance and were about to fall. The next horrible thing was to show you a can full of earth worms, blindfold you and then place a wet noodle in your mouth simulating a worm, "Yikes!" I yelled and spit it out of my mouth. Other things included being pelted with volley balls, and again, with an eye for safety, waist down only, and then finally, having your face painted.

I was in the American Bluejackets for approximately three years and learned a lot of things that helped me through Army training, like being yelled at by drill sergeants was no big deal. I think the petty officers training us in the Bluejackets were just as scary and tough on us as the Army drill sergeants, although the Army was a much more serious business given what we were preparing for, The Bluejackets were just about marching in parades such as the Memorial Day parade in Manhattan.

My father had worked for the Defense Department upon being discharged from the Army. He worked there for several years but left to get into a business venture partnership with a fellow government worker. As I recall it was a catering business called Rapid Caterers. As happens with many small businesses, Rapid

Caterers was not a success and went under. Dad went on to work several jobs before again being hired by the Defense Department as a Contracts Administer Procurement Officer. He was assigned to the Westhampton Air Force Base in Westhampton, Long Island, New York.

Because it was a very long commute from the Bronx to Westhampton my father decided to have a house built closer, so we moved to Patchogue, New York in July of 1962. Here again I had service people around me. We had an Air Force General at our house for dinner as well as a fighter pilot who was a lieutenant (I got that pronunciation right by this time), and a sergeant who was a WWII veteran and had completed twenty-five combat missions in Europe as a waist gunner aboard a B-17 bomber and had been shot down twice over the English Channel. He carpooled with my father daily so I saw him often. He loved watching the weekly TV program called *Twelve O' Clock High* and I loved hearing about his experiences.

After living in Patchogue for less than a year my parents separated. My mother, my younger sister, brother and I remained in the house in Patchogue. By this time, I had become friends with my next door neighbors. They had a cousin, Lenny Cook, who had a small sign business in Patchogue. Lenny had left for a time, owning and running a hunting lodge in Jonesport, Maine. Upon returning to Long Island, the hunting lodge having failed, he again started up his Cook Sign Company. I started working for Lenny part time after school during my senior year at Patchogue High School. Upon graduation I began working for Cook Sign Company on a full time basis. I had no benefits but the business kept improving and I learned a lot.

Leonard J. Cook was a hell of a guy. He was short in stature being about five-foot-six, and was well known around as a real scrapper if provoked but a fun guy when not. He was eight years my senior and I had the greatest time working for him and being his friend. He loved hunting but his brand of hunting was different from most. He talked me into some crazy stunts like hunting pheasant on the Suffolk County Honor penal farm with a very good chance of being caught by sheriff's deputies. On another occasion he talked me and another friend, Mike to hunt deer in Calverton, New York, right off the William Floyd Parkway. I said, "Are you nuts?" If we get caught it would mean a $500.00 fine.

He was adamant and told us, "If we get caught I'll pay the fines for you." So off we went to Calverton. We saw a deer standing on a knoll and Lenny shot it from the inside of his cousin Richie's 1957 Chevrolet. The first thing we did was drive back to Patchogue to drop off the shotgun. Lenny's instructions were, "If we got caught with the deer we claim that we found it. A search of the car would turn up no gun so we would be in the clear."

We went back, got the deer, and put it in the trunk of the car. Then back to Richie's house, and Lenny skinned and cleaned the deer. There are so many stories like this that I could write chapters about them. Lenny died at 48 years old, after living his life at 100 miles per hour. I will never forget Lenny.

While working at Cook Signs I met other guys who were to become my very good friends. Bill or "Willy," Mike, Billy and Jimmy. All who were Army except for Billy who was Coast Guard. The sign shop was a two car garage in the rear of Lenny's parents' house and had a double wide garage door we would leave open when the weather was warm. I was at the drawing board practicing some lettering when Willy arrived and drove his Harley Sportster right into the shop. The noise was deafening. He was asking, "Where is Lenny?"

As best as I could make out over the Harley's engine noise, I replied, "I don't know," more having Willy read my lips than actually being able to be heard over the motorcycle.

Willy began to work with us. He had been in the Army and was looking for steady work. While working alongside Willy, with the radio usually on, we heard the news that an American warship had been fired on in the Gulf of Tonkin. In retaliation, the U.S. was bombing the North Vietnamese PT Boat installations from where the attack craft had come from. I was cheering, "let's blow the hell out of them, who do they think they're messing with?"

Willy looked at me and said, "Don't cheer too much, you probably will be going." How does that saying go? "Truer words have never been spoken."

This happened in August of 1964, I was seventeen years old. The war escalated, and there was no indication that there would be a quick victory or resolution.

Chapter 2

Time went by and 1964, turned into 1965. In November of 1965, at 19 years of age, I was ordered by the local Selective Service office to report to Fort Hamilton in Brooklyn, New York for a physical. I followed instructions and arrived in my 1955 Chevy at the Selective Service System office located in Smithtown, New York along with twenty-five or so other guys. We boarded a yellow school bus for the trip to Fort Hamilton. I noticed that the sign above the bus's windshield read, "U.S. Government." Things were getting serious.

The physical exam was just as we had been told. We were herded from one area to another for various tests, most of which we had never been subjected to before. We had blood drawn, hearing tests, where you pressed a button on a device held by you whenever you heard a tone. Then there was the infamous rectal exam where the medic ordered you to "drop your drawers and bend over and spread them" while he inspected with the right angle Army flashlight. We were told that we would learn the overall results by mail. We went home wondering how much time we had left prior to being drafted into the US Army, currently at war in Vietnam.

Oddly, no one seemed scared or nervous about being drafted during a shooting war. The main concern or complaint was the interruption we would have to our lives and the family and girlfriends we would miss. School buses transported us back to Smithtown to where the Selective Service office was located in the same building as a real estate office. One of the guys joked that, "We're going to Vietnam to collect some real estate." We didn't realize that it was not going to be that kind of war.

After having completed the physical it became a waiting game as to what would happen next. Weeks passed and the letter arrived from Selective Service. I was upstairs in my bedroom and my mother called up saying, "You didn't pass the physical and you're 4F," meaning exempt from military duty due to some physical problem.

I said, "What, let me see that!"

She was kidding me because she knew I wanted to be a soldier. I knew she had mixed emotions. She was proud of me for wanting to serve but fearful having gone through the war in France. The Selective Service letter said to report for induction into the armed forces on January 19, 1966. Buses would take us from the Selective Service Office in Smithtown to Fort Hamilton in Brooklyn, just under the Verrazano Bridge that goes between Brooklyn and Staten Island, NY. There wouldn't be any return trip this day so Lenny Cook drove me to Smithtown and we said our goodbyes and good lucks.

Just about the same time, Joe Callahan, who was to become an Army buddy and who, I served with my entire Army time, was experiencing much the same thing being drafted out of Cleveland, Ohio.

Joe's experience in the US Army began on January 20, 1966. During the previous fall, Joe and his father were sitting on the front porch of their house at 1912 Elm Street when his cousin Danny Callahan drove by and stopped in front of the house. He didn't get out of the car but shouted up at them, "I just came from the draft board. I'm now 1-A" (available to be drafted). He also said that he mentioned to them that, "Joe is no longer attending school." Although Joe was not attempting to hide anything from the draft board he wanted them to ask about his school status rather than inform them. Not long after this incident he received his draft notice.

I wonder if Joe ever spoke to his cousin again.

Joe wasn't too concerned about the draft notice but his father was upset, this was unusual for him as he rarely showed emotion.

On January 20 Joe caught a morning train to Cleveland, (from the Erie Depot on Commerce Street) to be inducted into the US Army. His parents accompanied him to the station and that was the last he saw of them until after the completion of basic training a few months later in 1966.

At the induction center in Cleveland Joe joined a number of young men all receiving a physical exam. He filled out some paper work and found himself being sworn into the Army. He remembers that the group was asked for volunteers for the Marine Corps. They said that, "They would go to sunny and warm California for basic training." Since it was January and very cold that did catch Joe's attention. Also his father, his uncle Dan and cousins Jack and Bill Carney had all joined the Marines during WWII. However, he did not elect to go with the Marines to California and ended up on an older prop airplane heading to Fort Jackson, South Carolina. The inductees were told to memorize their serial numbers by the time they got to Ft. Jackson; Joe did and still remembers it, US52670876.

I had a health issue involving my gut called Irritable Bowel Syndrome or IBS. This is a condition that causes one to have intestinal pain and bathroom emergencies. There is no known treatment or cure. Doctors disagree as to whether or not it is caused by stress. I have had it since I was fifteen years old. I was wondering on the bus ride to Fort Hamilton if I would have to report sick so often I'd be sent home with a medical discharge. It has been a mystery for me and for doctors as to why I never once had a problem while in the Army. My brother Peter, who works at the American Museum of Natural History in New York City, happened to be on the phone with me one day while he was talking with a friend who is a psychiatrist. I heard him ask the doctor, "My brother has IBS but he never had it at all while he was in Vietnam. What do you think he should do? "the psychiatrist, without missing a beat, said, "Go back to Vietnam."

Chapter 3

Upon Arrival at Fort Hamilton in Brooklyn, New York the group I was with was herded into a large room with chairs set up theater-style. I think there were thirty or forty guys. Two sergeants were in charge, one Army and one Marine.

The Army sergeant got everyone's attention and said, "Out of this group we need nine Marines." He informed us that those selected to be Marines would be going to Parris Island and those selected to be Army would be going to Fort Jackson in South Carolina. He asked, "is there anyone who would opt and volunteer for the Marines?" No one did. Unlike Joe's experience, although similar, we were told, if no one volunteered nine people would be ordered into the Marines. I guess the age old words of wisdom in the military to "never volunteer" were already in play. My thoughts were clear; there was no way I was going to Parris Island...... Read on.

We were told to go to the cafeteria where there were box lunches available. We were told to, "Make sure you report back at thirteen-hundred hours or 1:00 PM in civilian time." Upon returning we were asked one at a time as we entered the room by the Army sergeant holding a clipboard, "Army or Marines?" Everyone including me said, "Army." At that point I thought I was home free from being drafted into the Marine Corps. Not so. Once everyone had returned the Army sergeant said, "Out of this group we need nine Marines, so the next nine names I call move to the other side of the room."

By this time, I already had a plan in place if called to be a Marine. I knew that until I was sworn in and had taken that one step forward I was a civilian. The military had no authority over me. I would refuse induction into the Marines but would make it clear that I was fully ready and willing to be drafted into the Army. The sergeants would make a big deal out of it; after all, they couldn't let this punk kid show such insubordination in front of the other recruits. They would probably threaten me with jail and fines that they really had no power to impose. So I would ask where the nearest public transportation off the post was and I would be on my way back home.

Now I have nothing but respect and admiration for the United States Marine Corps. My reason for preferring the Army was that my father had been in the Army, all my friends who had been in the military were Army and my uncle had been a paratrooper in the famed 82nd Airborne. I also wondered how a draftee would be received in the Marines who were traditionally all volunteers. Joe expressed the same concern.

Anyway, as it turned out I wasn't called for the Marines. Eight guys were called and one volunteered after his friend was called. They went off without making a peep. I hope they all did well in their time with the Marines. Sometime later we were lined up at attention and took the oath. With one ceremonious step forward we were officially recruits in the US Army. I was even sent to do some clerical work with the office staff.

The sergeant assigned one guy named Stuart to be in charge of the group and make sure we all made the train to Fort Jackson. We were bussed to the railway station in Manhattan, then had hours to kill before our train was to leave. I remember us all going to the Automat and getting some food. After boarding the train, we were assigned to sleeper cars for the overnight trip. I had never been in a sleeper car on a train and it was all new and exciting. We were awakened the next morning and sent to the dining car for breakfast. It was the first time any of us from the North had seen grits. The steward told us it was, "South Carolina snow." I didn't like it much.

It is hard to describe what any of us were feeling. Homesickness had not set in yet nor did any fear of what the future might hold. We all knew that at the end of the eight-week basic training we would get a two-week leave. Certainly we could hack eight weeks. Once we got a taste of the reception station we started to think, maybe not.

I was amazed that the train we were on took a siding that stopped directly within Fort Jackson. As soon as we got off the drill sergeants descended upon us with the hollering. We were "Meek Willys" who "couldn't sound off like we had a pair of balls" and the sergeants had, "grandmothers who could move faster than you." We were berated with not knowing the difference between right and left and, "your military right and left."

It was the American Bluejackets all over again. I had already gone through similar stuff so it didn't faze me; actually, I thought it was amusing. However, I would never let on to the drill sergeants that I wasn't scared lest they double their efforts with me.

The reception station was worse than basic training. We were made to stand in lines all day long in very cold weather. I thought South Carolina would be warm but it definitely was not. It was unusually cold for the region. One day it snowed, just a dusting, and the people who were regulars at Fort Jackson were running around just loving it. The reception center was under a strain because at this time 50,000 men a month were being drafted.

On our first night, and still in our civilian clothes, we were marched or, really not knowing how to march, herded through an area known as tent city. There were rows upon rows of eight-man tents, all on concrete bases. In the dark we were counted off one to eight and told to get inside. It was totally dark in there and we stood, not having been given any further instruction. One of the guys was tall and bumped his head into a bare light bulb hanging down from the top of the tent. He felt for the pull chain, found it and pulled. "Ah, let there be light." The guy was Michael Gittens who I went to high school with and whose family owned a produce stand about one block from my home in Patchogue.

Once we could see, we found a second bare bulb on the other end of the tent. There was also a small pot belly stove and a metal garbage can containing some wood boards, a small coal shovel and some coal. Mike used the shovel to shave some pieces of wood to use as kindling and after several attempts got the coal to ignite. Warmth at last. We were smart enough to set up a fire watch to keep the fire going all night, taking turns sleeping and stoking.

During this first night there was an incident that caused Sergeant Southby, who was commanding our group, to have the entire tent city fall out into ranks in the middle of the cold night. It was very dark and we couldn't see what was going on but he seemed to have one guy standing in front of the formation while screaming at him that he was a "raunchy bastard." We soon heard that the "raunchy bastard" had stepped outside the back of his tent and urinated rather than make his way down to the latrine. With many people living in close proximity we knew the Army took hygiene very seriously and we were sent back to our tents.

Upon Joe Callahan's arrival at Ft. Jackson very late in the day, around 10:00 or 11:00 PM, he went to what appeared to be a mess hall and completed numerous forms and tests. In the early morning his group was marched to some tents where they spent a few hours sleeping (without heat). They were later awakened to begin their first day in the Army. Joe got a haircut, was issued Army fatigues, and mailed his civilian clothes home. He spent a lot of time waiting, (SOP for the Army). He was then assigned to a barracks where he slept for the next couple of nights while he performed menial duties during the day such as policing the area (picking up bits of trash, etc.). He remembers having fire watch one night. Fire watch is conducted whereby a different soldier stays up for an hour in rotation with other soldiers in case there is a fire or other problem during the night, usually in barracks still having coal- fired pot belly stoves.

After a couple days at the reception center Joe was assigned to a basic training company, Company C, 2nd Battalion, 1st Training Brigade. Several more people arrived at the company area and made themselves "comfortable" in a row of old wooden barracks. Joe initially stayed in the last barracks at the bottom of a hill. Little by little others joined and eventually we were organized into a company. C or Charlie Company.

Joe writes: *there were several platoons (about 30 soldiers each) and each platoon had a drill sergeant in charge. Our sergeant was Sergeant Kunyer. Although I didn't know anyone I eventually met other soldiers and accepted the situation. One of my fellow soldiers was a guy from Patchogue, New York, (Long Island) named Pasquale or Pat Capainolo. Although we didn't know each other well during basic training we eventually became friends and spent the entire two years of Army life in the same units. We've kept in touch with each other through the years.*

The reception center had an area called "the shed." It really wasn't a shed at all but rather a large area covered by a roof and full of benches where you sat and waited for various things like haircuts, blood type testing, finger printing and getting dog tags. You always had to be "listening up" in case your name was called.

After you had your haircut, a two-minute buzz job, your head was very cold so many guys had towels wrapped around their heads. It was so cold that I saw people standing in line in front of one small building or another break ranks and try to get inside. It looked like something in a prisoner of war movie. By this time, and because of the cold, we were lined up and entered a shack, one at a time to get a plastic poncho and a hat. These were literally thrown into our faces! I saw one guy desperate to get warm try to squeeze into a shack only to be pushed back and knocked down the icy steps. The guy who pushed him was PFC Wells. Some shitheads you never forget.

The NCOs (Non Commissioned Officers) were in charge of the reception program but were helped by several PFCs. (Privates First Class). These PFCs, treated us miserably and certainly didn't live up to the sign we saw daily in front of the administration building saying "Welcome to the United States Army."

One of the recruits, braver than most, asked one of these PFCs where he was from. He said he was from New York. Most of us were also from New York, with a smattering from Philadelphia.

The recruit said, "We're from New York too and you treat us like this?" Believe it or not things improved with that one PFC. Was it a result of being from the same home town or fear that a rebellion was starting to bubble up?

By about the third day we were given our uniforms. These were very welcomed because they were much warmer than the civilian clothes we had worn up to this point. We were given some time to visit the PX (Post Exchange) so we could buy toiletries and over the counter remedies that the Army didn't issue. Unfortunately, that night, we heard ambulances coming to tent city. We heard through the rumor mill that some people had taken large amounts of over the counter drugs purchased at the PX in an effort to commit suicide.

I remember the dismal feelings I had that night. Not to the point of suicide but I still wondered: if I was dressed in civilian clothes and found the main gate could I just walk out? I had money I could use to get a cab ride to the closest rail station and buy a ticket for New York. I finally realized that if friends I knew went through this, I could too, and desertion was very serious business. It became a moot point anyway because the next day we had to ship all our civilian clothes home, probably to make desertion or AWOL that much harder to accomplish.

Joe had similar feelings, he writes, "*My initial feeling toward this change of life style was, I'm getting out of here! Army life was definitely not for me. But once you were in, it was not easy leaving. Actually, after I got to know some guys and we started basic training I totally forgot about getting out."*

The next day we had to return the poncho and hat we had been given since we now had uniforms. After turning in the items it was back under the shed. An NCO came with one of those endless clip boards and announced that the next names called would be boarding buses to travel to Fort Gordon, Georgia, for Basic Training. I was hoping I would be called, thinking any place would be better than this. I was not called and instead of getting on a bus we were loaded onto the Army's mainstay transportation, the two-and-a-half-ton truck known as the "deuce and a half." There were benches on both sides and one down the middle. We were made to squeeze in to make room, as the sergeants continued to yell, "Make your buddy smile." I hated that. Anyway, smiling or not, we headed up to Tank Hill.

Chapter 4

Tank Hill was a disappointment. Because of the name we expected to see a tank. You know, a tank with guns and treads and white stars painted on the sides. Instead it was a water tank. Not very interesting, although it did serve a purpose, however mundane. Once all of the trucks stopped we were ordered to jump down from the tailgate with our duffle bags and form up, four columns, toes on yellow lines painted on the street. Again with the clipboards, NCOs started calling names in alphabetical order, for barracks and bunk assignments.

Our First Sergeant was a WWII veteran who, according to his combat patch worn on the right shoulder, had been with the Third Infantry Division. This was Audie Murphy's outfit, the most decorated soldier of WWII. Our First Sergeant's name was Pavone and he had a Latino accent. He immediately started issuing orders to the NCOs, "Get those people inside the barracks and let them take any bunk available." I sensed that he did this because he knew how we had been subjected to standing in long lines for hours in the cold at the reception center.

Once inside we started feeling much better but thought it strange that we were left alone with no one screaming at us. We had no instructions or orders so we sat, got to know each other somewhat and wondered, "what next?" A soldier came up to tell us, "The mess hall is open and you can come down for mid-day chow." After eating we returned to the barracks and again just waited. Finally, we heard boots resonating on the wooden stairs and into the barracks came Drill Sergeant Kunyer. I had seen Sergeant Kunyer pacing on the deck around the administration building with several other drill sergeants who looked at us like we were fresh meat. He seemed to me to be the least threatening looking so I was glad to be assigned to his platoon. The sergeant told us, "You are in my platoon and my name is Kunyer, pronounced *koonya.*" He said, "You have the rest of the day off. However, you are confined to barracks. Training will start tomorrow morning. There is no smoking or eating in the barracks."

The next morning, we were awakened by the CQ or "Charge of Quarters", and after breakfast we were given our barracks and bunk assignments. Like so many other things in the Army we were assigned in alphabetical order. I ended up with a bottom bunk and the guy above me was a fellow by the name of Brian Burns. He had been drafted after graduation from college, having been on a student deferment. He was from Nyack, New York and his father was an NYPD detective. We traded horror stories of the reception center and I told the story of everybody being rousted out of bed in the middle of the night due to the actions of one "raunchy bastard." Brian smiled. "Can you believe it? I was the "raunchy bastard." We had a good laugh and became friends.

I didn't find basic training as hard as it was cracked up to be. My early cadet training paid off, and learning close order drill or the manual of arms or the spit and polish required for your uniforms was fairly simple. Physically, it was demanding with forced marches and constant "double timing" or trotting in ranks.

Chapter 5

Everyone I knew or met who had had Basic Combat Training or, "BCT"at Fort Jackson knew of "Drag Ass Hill". It was a washout or gulley going up to the water tank that was about waist deep and five or six feet wide. We had to run up that gulley almost daily. My greatest fear was to fall out during running double time, having seen what happened to another trainee who did.

We were double timing on a road with rifles at "port arms", that is with rifles held across our chest with muzzle to the left and wearing steel helmets. One guy dropped out to the side of the road out of breath, looking spent. The drill sergeant called "platoon halt." Two trainees were singled out and the sergeant ordered, "You two pick up his rifle and get him on his feet." We resumed our double timing; the two trainees were literally dragging him along. I thought the guy was going to die of a heart attack.

The word was that since each recruit had gone through a physical examination and was deemed fit for training; the drill sergeants were not held responsible if someone actually died. We later heard that a guy in Echo Company did die of a heart attack while doing a one-mile running test.

It turned out that I had a friend from back home in Patchogue who had joined the Army. When we met up in the Consolidated Mess Hall I learned he was in Echo Company, and he found out I was in Charlie Company, both in the second training battalion of the first training brigade. His name was Tony Nirow.

One Saturday I was sitting in the barracks playing cards on a foot locker with some of my buddies when I heard someone asking, "Is Capainolo in these barracks?" Two guys were directed to me. One was Tony Nirow, who I knew was in Echo company, and the other guy was a lifelong friend who had lived two doors away from me in the Bronx. His name was Anthony Marcosi. We met for hamburgers at an on post cafeteria. Another guy joined with them, also from my home in Patchogue, New York; his name, as I recall, was Carl Frost. So far I'd met four people I knew. Having friends there made it feel like I was less alone.

There were times when we would have some laughs. Right after lights out someone might call out to another, "Brian, you give a shit?" Brian would answer, "No, you?" then someone else would chime in, "Hey, Capainolo, you give a shit?" I would answer Nah, you?" Someone else called out, "Hey, Callahan, you give a shit?" Callahan answered "No, you?" This went on for about a half hour until everyone dropped off to sleep.

One day, after firing our rifles, we of course had to clean them. Sergeant Broward, as I recall was going through the ranks, inspecting each trainee's rifle. We kept hearing the same old thing: "your rifle barrel is as dirty as a dirt road," or, "You could grow carrots in there." It would behoove you to keep your weapons clean. "Behoove" being a staple Army term used ad nauseam. Tiresome stuff always until Burns failed inspection and got chided for it. He said to Sergeant Broward, "Hey, sarge, ask me if I give a shit." Sergeant Broward went for it and asked, "Do you give a shit?" Burns responded, "Nah, I don't give a shit, you?" The whole platoon cracked up until the sergeant ordered us to attention. I don't remember Burns being disciplined for this but I can't say for sure. Burns was already a respected guy, him being twenty-three years old and the rest of us eighteen and nineteen.

What I particularly remember about Sergeant Broward was how large his head was. It looked like he had to press his helmet liner on with a pop. The one time I had a run in with him was a day when he caught me not having shaved that one morning. He said the same things we had heard about a million times: "Next time you shave take one step closer to the razor." Or: "What did you do this morning, shave through a screen door?" Anyhow, he got me on the parade field and told me to report to him during the break. When the break came he was standing and gabbing with a major. I didn't want to get the attention of the major so I waited until their conversation was over. At that same instant the break was over. So now I was guilty of disobeying an order. Sergeant Broward gave me a choice: "Go talk with the major or clean the grease trap in the mess hall." Naturally, I took the grease trap. Although, thinking back, I should have called his bluff. Would he *really* take me up to the major for such a trivial matter? If he did it might have backfired on him, with the major chiding him for not being able to handle a small disciplinary matter with a lowly recruit. I should have tried it but I was not yet Army protocol or politically astute. But I was learning.

The grease trap was a kind of an underground concrete catch basin outside and back of the mess hall. It was half filled with water and somehow the grease from the drains floated to the top. So you had to lie on your belly and scoop the grease out using a ladle. Your uniform would get so much slimy grease on it all you could do was throw it out. Your boots, that had to be kept shined all the time, were coated with a fine layer of grease and had to be worked on for an hour to get them to shine again.

Lucky for me the grease trap had already been done by some other unfortunate rule breaker. So I was given other kitchen duties like scrubbing the stove tops with a lemon half. Not that bad

One of the cooks was named SP/5 Stowe. He was mean as hell on the KP's. He would scream and berate them all day. He had a PFC helper named Lloyd who was just as bad, maybe worse. One incident I saw made me feel quite a lot better about our drill sergeants. There was a soldier who was not in my platoon but had KP as well. He was sick with a cold or sore throat or what was called "recruits' disease." Recruits Disease was an upper respiratory infection, and the Army figured that a large percentage of trainees would get sick from being out in the elements for long hours. Regulations supposedly called for any recruit missing three day's training would be recycled to a company that was behind our training schedule. There he could pick up where he had left off. No one wanted that.

The soldier reported to SP/5 Stowe that, "I'm sick and need to go on sick call." As usual he was looked upon as being a malingerer. One of his buddies saw how sick he was and reported it to his drill sergeant. The drill sergeant as I remember was thin and kind of smallish. He confronted SP/5 Stowe and told him, "I'm taking my trainee to sick call." Well, there were some words exchanged and the drill sergeant jumped over the railing where you slide your tray along and got right in Stowe's face. He called for his soldier and told him, "I'm taking you to the dispensary right now." Stove just stood there. Hmmm… let's see, drill sergeant vs. cook, no contest. The word got around that Stowe almost got his ass kicked, and there was a new found respect for our drill sergeants. It made us feel and understand that the drill sergeants were tough so we would learn what we needed to survive combat, but they would also back us up.

I too, succumbed to recruits disease. I got the worst sore throat you could imagine. I was sent to the hospital, worried about getting recycled and a new threat, spinal meningitis. Spinal meningitis was a sickness you could die from and here I was in an Army hospital. One symptom of spinal meningitis was that you could not lower your chin to your chest due to swelling at the base of your skull. The medics and nurses came around regularly and had us perform this test. I did it so much that my neck did become sore and the thought of it being fatal crossed my mind.

I remember having the sweats and shivering. I asked the nurse making her rounds if I could have another blanket. She said no, "It's against hospital rules." Whoa! A regular Nurse Ratchet from *"One Flew Over the Cuckoo's Nest."* So each day after her rounds, I took an extra blanket from an empty bed. The doctor would come to the ward and stand at the entrance with two aides and a small cart containing various drugs and medical implements. No matter how sick we were we had to stand in single file with our dog tags thrown over our backs so the doctor could use his stethoscope on our chest. One guy got an injection and promptly fell down on the deck while on his way back to his bunk. The doctor and his aides ran over and did whatever they needed to and revived him.

Fortunately, I recovered enough to return to my company, having spent one weekday and two weekend days in the hospital. The weekend days did not count as training days so I didn't get recycled. Once discharged from the hospital I walked back to my Company area. Having my boots back on felt terrific. I asked around and found my Company on the parade field stripped down to their waists. It was February and very cold. I found the sergeant in charge or, "NCOIC" and told him, "I've just been released from the hospital and don't think stripping to the waist in freezing cold is the thing to do."

He replied, "If you were released without light duty orders you are fit for training."

Once the day and chow was over I was real glad to get into my barracks. I looked around and saw canvas shelter halves tied to each end of the bunks creating kind of a train sleeping car affect. These were called "sneeze sheets" and were supposed to prevent contamination from one soldier to another. The old wood windows were nailed open about a half inch from the bottom. This was supposed to keep the recruits from closing them and defeating the purpose of keeping the barracks aerated.

In my barracks there were two guys who evidently kept screwing up. I didn't really see what they were doing wrong, but whatever it was it got them recycled and transferred to the "motivation platoon." We had heard some scary stories about this special platoon. It was made up of trainees from various companies who were having trouble "getting with the program" which was another admonition we heard many, many times. I saw those two guys just once more and heard what they were going through. It was the same training as ours except they got much more harassment than we did. Of course, the word was that the Army didn't do any harassment. Well, then let us call it very intense, in your face, one on one negative reinforcement. I don't know what became of them, just two more guys caught up in the "big green machine."

We received training on the Manual of Arms. This, for the uninitiated, was the handling of rifle commands like, right shoulder arms, left shoulder arms, present arms, etc. Since I had three years in the Bluejackets carrying a rifle most of the time I was proficient in these skills. We trained on a flat, open parade ground. I was amused to see people who had a hard time executing the commands. During a smoke break I helped some guys learn the drill, and just to show off, I did some of the trick drill stuff you might see honor guards doing at ceremonies.

Sergeant Kunyer saw this going on, and when the break was over we were ordered to fall into ranks. The sergeant called me to "front and center." He ordered me to "attention" and began giving me commands. I did them well and he tried an old trick on me. He called me to "present arms" and I executed the movement. He then called me to "right shoulder arms." I didn't move; rather I stayed frozen at present arms. He smiled and knew right off that I was aware that the only command you were allowed to follow from present arms was order arms. Once at order arms you could then follow any other command. The sergeant's intent was to show the platoon that if Capainolo can do it so can you. Anyway, it was a proud moment for me.

The main Army rifle used at the time was the M-14, while in my cadet days we used the 1903 Springfield, touted to be a better rifle for drill as it was better balanced. Looking at five armed services I found that some of the rifle drill teams currently use the 1903 Springfield. This rifle is a bolt action rifle that fires 30.06 caliber rounds and was adopted by the Army way back in 1903 and was still in use, mainly by the Marines, in the Pacific, during the early days of the Second World War.

After several weeks we noticed that trainees from other companies had ear plugs attached to their epaulettes. They were in small plastic vials like the ones prescription medicines come in, except they were clear and had a small beaded chain affixed to them. The earplugs meant they were in rifle training.

When our turn came we were issued our own ear plugs and marched to the rifle range. Wow, we were finally going to do something fun. The first thing we saw was a sergeant giving us a talk about recoil and that it wasn't really bad. To demonstrate he held a rifle butt against his genitals with the muzzle held high into the air and fired. He didn't flinch. I found out he wore a sports protective cup for this demonstration and the recoil was in fact substantial. We were firing M-14 rifles and the rounds were 7.62 mm. The idea was to not anticipate the rifle's report.

I had fired rifles and shot guns before but never had any instruction. Once on the firing range we were each assigned a "field of fire" or a lane. We were shown different firing positions, some of which were hard to achieve unless we were very flexible. The target was the typical bull's eye except it had an inch square drawn just on top of the bull's eye. You had to get three rounds into the square in a tight pattern. Looking through the iron sights of the rifle you couldn't make out the one-inch square but could see the target's bull's eye. You fired at the bull's eye but the bullets struck the square. What was going on here? As best as I understood it was that, at a close range the bullet would rise. Well it didn't. What was happening? You must remember the rifle wasn't aimed by looking directly down the inside or barrel of the weapon. The sights are affixed to the top of the barrel, so you must compensate for that by aiming just a tad lower than your target.

The range sergeants ran this part of your Basic Training. You were ordered to take the prone position, keep your weapon pointed down range, and lock and load using your twenty round magazine with only three rounds in it. Each firing position had a wide wooden stake driven into the ground with a number on it. That was your lane, and the rifle could be rested on it with the muzzle on top of the wood and the butt sitting on the ground while resting between firing. The range instructors held up a red paddle when you were not supposed to be firing and a green paddle when you were to commence firing. You were trained to remember the acronym "B.R.A.S.S." that stood for breath, relax, aim, sight picture, and squeeze. Words to live by for hitting your target.

The paddles were about the size of a tennis racquet. Once you were ordered to hold your fire the instructors would get the targets and see how you did. The instructor who was monitoring my group of trainees said to me, "Good shooting, Capainolo, except that you shot up your buddy's target and never touched yours," *Embarrassing.* After that I stayed in my firing lane but, for some reason, I was not doing well with hitting the target in a tight pattern. I couldn't see very well with my glasses on because gun oil kept spritzing on them with the rifle's recoil. Joe Callahan had the same problem. I got rid of the glasses since I found they were not helping. Still having problems, I was sought out by First Sergeant Pavone who of course asked, "Capainolo, are you blind? You better get with the program, you skinhead, dammit."

By this time, I figured out that the adjustable sights on my rifle were moving due to the recoil. I told this to Sergeant Pavone who said, "Let me see that weapon and find out if you know what you are talking about." He opened the butt plate at the end of the rifle and pulled out a tool that he used to tighten the sights. Problem solved except the First Sergeant wasn't totally convinced so he kept checking up on me and when the day came to "fire for record" he put me into a special group of trainees who needed to be closely monitored. I felt like a jerk and didn't belong there since after the sight tightening I was shooting just fine.

Firing for record was a big deal; after all, we were soldiers. The process was you were given one hundred rounds of ammunition to shoot down ninety-six "killable" targets spaced out from twenty-five to three-hundred meters. The targets were silhouettes of a man from the waist up. The target would stay up for a short time, then a horn would blow and the targets would go down. So you had to aim and fire quickly as well as accurately. Each shooter had a scorer who would make sure you were firing from the right positions and keep track of your kills. Most of the firing was from a fox hole, resting your rifle at about shoulder level, leaning the barrel on sandbags. However, a portion of the shooting had to be done from one of the positions you learned on the rifle range. You had a choice as to which position you would use. I chose the kneeling position as opposed to the squatting or prone positions.

Of the ninety-six targets you had to kill a minimum of thirty to be scored as a "Marksman," thirty-one to fifty-nine to be "Sharpshooter" and sixty or more to be "Expert" I managed a score of fifty-six, just short four targets from "Expert." Since you were given one hundred rounds you were allowed to fire on any target twice and use up the extra four rounds if you could do so before the horn went off and the target dropped. To this day I still regret not getting "Expert" and that the reason was I didn't use what I had learned while in training; Remember, if the target is close, aim low. With the killable targets this meant at waist level, which was the very bottom of the target. The rest of the target just sat there, and looking big at just twenty-five meters I couldn't resist firing at the chest level. Good thing it wasn't a mistake made in combat; the bullet would have just whizzed over the enemy's head.

Anyway, we were given our rifle badges to be worn on our dress uniforms for the rest of our time in the Army. Your score was kept in your personal file

One of the more fun things we did was being lined up and assigned foxholes ten abreast. In front of us was an open dirt field. We were told that when the targets came up they would be timed like an advancing group of enemy soldiers. We were to fire a full twenty round magazine without aiming, just point and fire away. It was an exercise to see what a squad of riflemen could do in laying down fire. This was eye opening, and Joe Callahan and I were laughing and choking on the gun smoke we had created.

Chapter 6

Now that we could fire the rifle, what about the bayonet affixed to it? Well, there was a whole lot of training that went into that. Something we would hear throughout this phase of training was, "There are only two kinds of bayonet fighters, the quick and the dead." Most of the training dealt with running at a target, rifle held out straight, and piercing a straw dummy with the bayonet. There was also training on close combat against an enemy trying to kill you with a bayonet. Parry left and parry right were moves you made to deflect the opponent's bayonet coming at you. Another thing we heard was that if you bayoneted someone you would never pull the trigger to extract the bayonet. This was something only done in the movies. The sergeant would say, "Why in the hell would you bayonet someone if you had a round in your rifle?"

Why indeed?

We also learned how to use the rifle to deliver vertical and horizontal butt strokes to our opponent's heads and had training with what was called pugil sticks. This was a round wood shaft approximately four feet long and padded at both ends. You and your opponent wore protective equipment and football helmets. You banged away at each other using what we had learned in bayonet training. I don't think the intention was to hone your bayonet skills but rather to whet your aggression. Many soldiers never had been involved in a physical fight and found it hard to attack another person.

Get over it.

I had read somewhere that the US Army was thinking of doing away with bayonets entirely. Statistically, they counted for few enemy casualties. Also, with the M-16 coming into use another bayonet mount would have to be designed for use with the new rifle. That would be an expensive move for the Defense Department. It was finally determined that the bayonet would remain in service as more of a psychological weapon than as a practical weapon in modern warfare. When the order was given to "fix bayonets" you were pretty sure it meant "do or die, there will be no retreat." When the enemy became aware that you were fixing bayonets they now knew they were facing a dug-in, hardened opponent, who would not back off.

Theoretically.

To add to all the fun and excitement we had a drill intended to familiarize ourselves with the gas masks we had to carry everywhere. We trained on the gas mask's use and how to properly put it on. To warn everyone that there was a gas attack in progress you had to bang metal on metal. In order to put a mask on properly, you would place your rifle between your legs, butt on the ground, and put your helmet over the muzzle so you had both hands free to put on the gas mask.

We were made to enter a tent with tear gas in it, take our gas masks out of their pouches, put them on and clear them. There were several straps on the gas mask that you pulled tight to secure it to your face. Once the instructor was satisfied that you had put the mask on the right way and you were not gagging he pulled it off. We were told, "O.K, now state your name, rank, serial number and date of birth." Of course, once the gas hit your face it felt like acid. The burning was intense. We were advised, "Just leave the tent and face into the wind until the effect wears off." My face, lips and eyes burned so bad I was sure some mistake was made and I would suffer permanent damage. I didn't.

We learned how to and how not to throw hand grenades. You don't throw them with a stiff arm extended like you see in old John Wayne movies. You threw them as you would a baseball. I had plenty of practice throwing dummy grenades at targets but missed out on the live grenade throw since I was in the hospital at that time. My friends told me it was kind of scary once you pulled the pin. The modern hand grenades were smooth rather than the old WWII and Korean War "pineapple" type.

Chapter 7

A character we met was a prior service guy named Bell. He was thirty-eight years old and having a really hard time keeping up with the rigors of physical training. He was small and thin but badly out of shape, too old for double timing it up "drag ass hill." Bell was taken out of the normal training exercises and became a permanent "CQ" or Charge of Quarters. CQ was someone who manned the Company office all night and answered any telephone calls that came in. You had to answer each call with, in my case as an example, "165th Transportation Company PFC Capainolo speaking, sir." You had to say sir, just in case it was an officer, but it rattled the caller, be they family or friends by sounding so official. The CQ would go to the individual's barracks and get him for the call. The CQ also woke everyone up in the morning, starting with the day's KPs (Kitchen Police) at 3:00 A.M. and the rest of the troops at 5:00 AM. The KPs were identified by tying a white towel to the head of their bunks. In the Army the word "Police" usually meant cleaning up.

We began to notice when Bell seemed to have CQ duty quite often he would come in the morning, flip the light switches on and off and yell, "Get your feets on the floor" … not the most educated soldier. Next we saw him sporting new "mosquito wings,'' Army speak for Private First Class single chevrons on the sleeves of his uniform. How did he get to be a PFC? Well, it turns out the Army is more compassionate than most people would guess. In all probability, Bell couldn't make it on the outside so he came back to the Army for the steady pay and benefits. He could have been discharged for not passing the tests we all had to pass so the Army made him "permanent party" as he called it. Good for Bell, I hope he did well, "Get your feets on the floor" and all.

Speaking of education; almost all of us were just high school graduates with little or no college. We did have some guys who were Officer Candidates and were distinguishable as such by a white vertical stripe on the back of their helmets or helmet liners. They would have had more education than the average recruit in my company. I remember speaking with a guy from Georgia, not an OCS candidate, who kept going on about the South shall rise again and the Confederates vs. the Yankees and all of that kind of banter. It was all good natured. I asked him how it felt to be in the very Army that defeated the Confederacy. He looked at me and said in all seriousness, "What do you mean? The Yankees all had blue uniforms."

We had an interesting mess sergeant whose name escapes me now, and even if I did remember it I wouldn't use it, he was that frightening. He was a large black man with a lot of stripes on his sleeves. He would walk around the tables during chow saying, "Eat up, eat up, shitbirds, swallow it, chew it later." He had a curious way of saying that everything was his rather than the Army's. For instance, one time I was picked to be a server on the chow line, Burns was also a server, standing right next to me. I don't remember what exactly I was serving but I do remember Burns was serving Jello. The mess sergeant came up behind Burns, observed the portions he was spooning out, and said in his big booming voice, "Don't you be given' away all my Jello, I 'll kill your ass." Burns just froze.

As it happened, when we went out on bivouac, I paired up with Joe Callahan. After the long march we shared a two-man tent for the night. The way these tents worked was that each soldier carried a "shelter half," or half of a "pup tent" as civilians would call it. You paired up with a soldier who had either buttons or zippers to match your own and joined the two halves making a full tent. After some initial confusion over buttons or zippers we settled down for the night. It was raining. Joe and I used our small shovels, called entrenching tools, and dug a small drainage ditch around the bottom of the tent to divert the water flowing down the sides of the tent. An engineering marvel. Sometime during the course of the night I had to visit the latrine. As I walked into the unlit latrine I saw two figures sitting on toilets both wearing their gas masks. They looked like two aliens with big bug eyes and long snoots.

The next day it was still raining and I was picked to go back to our Company area after dinner to be ready for KP the next morning. I had to report to the field mess and get on a deuce and a half truck that would be going back to our company area. Before leaving, we were instructed to turn our rifles over to the armorer who had racks full of rifles belonging to people on KP or other duties back at our regular Company area. The rifle was completely wet due to the rain. I handed it to one of the armorers and told him, "The rifle needs to be dried and oiled so it won't rust."

He took the rifle and said, "Yeah, we'll take care of it."

I got to sleep in my own barracks and bunk that night only to be awakened at 3:00 AM. I was assigned to the back sink which was the least desirable job on KP. You had to clean and scrub the big pots and pans at a rapid pace. Also, the mess sergeant kept making the water hot to the touch. There was no dish washing soap. We used brown soap cut in hunks and placed in coffee cans with holes drilled through the bottom to create some suds.

KP was harder than usual because, following bivouac, we would be graduating basic training. The mess hall had to be completely cleaned before the new training cycle started. In addition, we had to truck the food out to the bivouac area to serve chow out of large insulated containers and return after the evening meal to the Company area to clean or "GI" everything. (To GI something means to clean and scrub). The immersion heaters were a whole other job in themselves. They were gasoline or diesel fed contraptions, with a fire box immersed in water-filled metal garbage cans. There were usually three of these set up in a row with a big brush tethered to each one. The troops would first scrape their trays or mess kits into the garbage then dip and scrub them in each successive boiling can of water, starting with the soapy water, and ending with the rinse water.

It was a very long day, and to top it off, we found that someone had forgotten to pick up the next group of KPs so we would be on again the next day! Very bad news. During the course of the second day on KP, I was called to the Company armory. The armory sergeant pulled a rifle off its place in the weapons rack and slammed it down on top of his counter. It was badly rusted and he asked, "Is this you rifle?" I said, "No sergeant, my rifle doesn't look anything like that." He picked up the rifle turned it to where he could read the serial number and told me to, "State your rifle serial number." Sure enough it was mine.

I said, "When I was pulled off bivouac I turned my rifle over to the armory guys. They told me that they would take care of it."

He didn't seem to care, he told me, "Get that rifle cleaned and oiled in ten minutes or you'll be in serious trouble."

While I was frantically cleaning the rifle, the "Eat up, shitbirds" mess sergeant came in looking for his lost KP. He told me, "Get back to the mess hall or I'll kill your ass."

The armory sergeant said, "He isn't going anywhere until that rifle is inspection ready."

The two sergeants began arguing over whether I went back to the mess hall or stayed and cleaned the rifle. Something told me I had better get that rifle cleaned and oiled before they turned their collective wrath on me.

While they got into each other's face, I hurriedly got the rifle squared away. With the two sergeants still glaring at each other the armory sergeant was satisfied with the rifle's restoration and I double-timed it back to the mess hall.

Working on the pots and pans with very hot water had burned my finger nail beds and I couldn't continue putting my hands into the hot water. I explained it to the cook in charge but he didn't believe me. I was fed up by now with the relief KPs having been forgotten, the rifle incident and the burned fingernails. I stood my ground and said, "I want to go to the dispensary." That seemed to make him think twice; perhaps he remembered the incident between Stowe, the cook, and the drill sergeant? He put me on dining room orderly or, "DRO," where I didn't have to submerse my hands in hot water.

One of the KPs asked, and got permission, to walk down to the dry cleaners to get his dress uniform for the graduation ceremony to be held the next morning. While walking, a jeep stopped with a colonel in the passenger seat.

The colonel asked, "Why are you not with the rest of the battalion in the field on bivouac?"

The soldier told him, "I'm on KP and I'm going down to the cleaners to get my uniform. The colonel asked, "Why didn't you get it yesterday, knowing you would be on KP today?"

The soldier replied, "I was on KP yesterday too because someone forgot to bring in the relief KP's for today."

The colonel was very interested in that, and visited Charlie Company to kick a few butts around. Our Company officers were not too happy with the soldier who had spoken with the colonel.

Graduation from Basic Combat Training was a ceremony where we all wore our dress greens with garrison hats rather than service caps, bloused boots and a pistol belt. We thought we looked really cool with boots bloused like paratroopers. The pistol belt was worn so we could attach our bayonet scabbards and bayonets. The entire battalion was on parade and we marched in review, passing the stands where there were many parents of graduating soldiers. The officer calling out the commands had a hard time being loud enough and his voice broke several times when he ordered, "Atten'hut, fix bayonets, pre...esent haarms," but we had practiced enough to know what he was saying. We fixed bayonets and followed the manual of arms commands, managing not to cut or stab anyone. It was a proud day and I noticed the drill sergeants now called us soldier or trooper rather than skin heads and shitbirds.

Author-Graduation from Basic Combat Training

After changing back into our fatigues we had a beer party. It was held at a wood building I had never seen before in an area that looked like a civilian park or picnic area. I was sitting with a couple of guys drinking some beer and we were joined by the mess sergeant who still intimidated us. One of our buddies came over and said something like, "What are you jerks doing"?

True to form the mess sergeant looked at him and said, "Don't you be callin' my soldier's names, I'll kill your ass."

I heard some kind of commotion coming from a building nearby and went over to see what it was. The PFC cook who had given all of us a very nasty time when on KP was in a fist fight with two or three soldiers. I saw a beer can bounce off his head. Two drill sergeants stood by for a while before interceding. It appeared they knew of the bad treatment this guy had subjected KP's to while in his charge and thought a bit of a beating was justified.

Eight weeks and basic training was over. Joe was on his way back to Youngstown, Ohio on a Greyhound bus (a long trip), and I was on my way back by train to Patchogue, New York, an equally long trip. After returning to Youngstown, Joe wrote, "*I was met by my parents, sister, and cousin Danny, who was still a civilian but would eventually be drafted. He spent most of his Army time in Germany and wrote to me several times. Germany, it figures; remember he was the guy who told the draft board that I was out of school. I hope he had a good time in Germany probably visiting Paris, Italy and Switzerland as well. Pat and I visited Cam Ranh Bay, South Vietnam and Sattahip Thailand; both smelled so bad new guys would throw up. However, we did get to go to Bangkok. and Pataya, Thailand.*"

Everybody at both of our respective homes thought that we looked much healthier than before basic; perhaps the uniform made an impression.

Chapter 8

We started getting our written orders as to where we were to report next and at what location. Nearly everyone got orders for some kind of technical training rather than advanced infantry where you trained to be a rifleman. When you first entered basic training you were given a battery of tests. Some of the questions were, "Do you consider yourself as being rugged? Do you enjoy camping?" I answered no to questions like that. I believed scoring yes to those questions put you on a path to infantry. Maybe they didn't, but it was strange to me why a guy like Burns who had graduated college got orders for infantry.

With the coming of our individual assignments there was a lot of buzz in the air. Everyone was comparing orders and asking the sergeants what the heck some of them even meant. Training was over, and we became more relaxed. The whole platoon was told to attend a meeting to further our understanding of what the technical assignments meant, and got briefed as to when we could start our two-week leave.

We were told in no uncertain terms that regardless of what our MOS; "Military Occupational Specialty" was we were all riflemen first. The speaker went on to warn us that Vietnam was not like WWII or Korea; there were no front lines and you could be killed anywhere at any time. His statements were sobering...

I went on my two-week leave taking a train from Columbia, South Carolina to New York City and out to Long Island. It was great being home again and seeing all my family and friends. I even went on some sign hanging jobs. I noticed right away I could scamper up ladders with ease, being in great shape after all of the double-timing and exercising I had done.

The leave was over too soon and I found myself boarding a train at Pennsylvania Station heading to Augusta, Georgia. I reported to the in-processing desk and presented my orders to the clerks. They looked at the orders, checked some clipboards (no computers then) and made some telephone calls. My orders were for Marine Engine Maintenance and Repair at Fort Gordon, Georgia.

One small problem: there was no Marine Engine Maintenance and Repair at Fort Gordon. My orders were screwed up and should have been cut for Fort Eustis in Newport News, Virginia. Just great.

So I was sent over to what was called Administration Company where I met about twenty guys awaiting their new orders. We all kind of lived out of our duffle bags. A few of the guys had completed communication training and they would practice their Morse Code calling out dots and dashes for half the night. We had no idea what they were saying. We were kept on a list where we were picked each day to do various jobs on the post. I got stuck with painting barracks ceilings.

Those of us who were painting were given old fatigues to wear over our own. They were already paint spattered. We hated the painting because there were no finished ceilings. You were looking at the floor boards of the barracks above us. There was a lot of crisscrossing support pieces making painting difficult. I took some white paint and painted a P on my back like a prisoner of war. We all had a laugh but when the NCO came back to check on our progress he was not happy about it and I got chewed out. No big deal; it was good for a laugh while doing some very boring work.

Somehow, on the next day, I was taken off the painting detail. If you didn't get put on a detail you just hung around the barracks. That's how I met some of the other soldiers. One guy had orders for air frame repair. He was from Florida. Another one I met was Jaffe. He was a cool little guy and reminded me of Woody Allen. We all stayed in our fatigues but he liked to wear his khakis. He used to wear his service cap rather than the garrison hat. He would take the stiffener out of the hat that kept it round. He then bent the two sides down to what was called the "sixty mission bend." The sixty mission bend was how pilots wore the service cap. The bend was caused by wearing a communications head set over and across the hat. This hat style was considered out of uniform for regular troops. But no matter how many times Jaffe was told to put the stiffener back in, he invariably would take it out again as soon as no one was around to enforce the uniform code.

Finally, someone came into our Administration barracks and called out the names of individuals whose new orders could be picked up at the administration office. The next morning a few guys and I took up our duffel bags and headed to the office. Once announced, I was given an envelope containing my new orders. The orders told me to report to Fort Eustis located near Newport News, Virginia. As it turned out the air frame repair guy also had orders for Fort Eustis and had brought his car from his home in Florida to Fort Gordon. The sergeant who was in charge of providing transportation for anyone leaving Fort Gordon flipped out, "What are you doing bringing your own car when you were told leaving Basic that you couldn't get your car on your new post until authorized?" Once he calmed down he said, "I'm not supposed to do this but I am going to change your transportation orders to POV, personally owned vehicle, then he said, "Why not let some of these other people going to Fort Eustis ride with you and share expenses?" We all readily agreed, thanking the sergeant. "You're a life saver, sergeant, we thought we would have to leave the car here."

Chapter 9

The air frame soldier, myself and someone named Honeybee from a tiny town in Tennessee all rode together in a 1961 Chevy from Augusta, Georgia to Newport News, Virginia. The ride was great until we went through a speed trap somewhere in South Carolina.

A police officer driving a big Pontiac patrol car put his lights on behind us so we pulled over. The officer came up to the driver's door and told the driver to, "Get out and go stand by my patrol car." He gave the remaining two of us a quick look, went back to his car and told our driver to, "Get in." Luckily, we were all in uniform and figured that might factor in to whatever was going to happen. He kept the driver for about a half-hour and finally let him go back to his car.

Once back in the driver's seat he told us that the police officer just gave him a lengthy speech and a warning not to speed. I don't know if the uniforms were much help.

So we were on our way. Since we had a long drive we decided to get a hotel room to stay overnight in Raleigh, North Carolina. Here again the uniforms didn't help much. The hotel clerk asked us, "What are your plans? I hope you're not having a drinking party. I don't want to clean up a mess a few drunks could make."

We assured her that was not the case and she gave us the room. We ate dinner at the Raleigh Hotel and looked at the pamphlets at the front desk. We saw one advertising "Jim Thorpe's Discothèque." It was close by so we went.

The discotheque was a barn with bleachers and a wood basketball court where people danced. The music was primarily country with some rock tunes sprinkled in. The people there were mostly young, and apart from a few curious looks no one bothered with us. At this time in history the anti-war movement had not really heated up yet and we didn't have any trouble. After our pleasant night at the Raleigh Hotel we were on the road again headed for Fort Eustis. The 1961 Chevy rode very nicely and we knew we were close when we got near Jamestown on the James River. We had to cross the James River by ferry and Honeybee was afraid, never having seen this big a body of water in his whole life. He also wanted to know what those big birds flying around were. He was awed by the seagulls. Scared or not, we all got on board the ferry and crossed the river with no problem.

We had no difficulty in following the road signs to Fort Eustis and entered the post at the main gate where the MP's (Military Police) directed us to where we would process in.

Chapter 10

Fort Eustis, Virginia, is the home of the US Army Transportation Corps. As such it was the home of the Army's Transportation School and I was to train there for Marine Engine Maintenance and Repair. The post was pleasant enough and seemed a step up from Fort Jackson. The barracks we occupied were masonry rather than wood and the training facilities were neat and kept very clean. By us, of course.

Technical school was not physically demanding like field exercises. Each day we received training with various marine diesel engines. We also learned some shipboard electrical systems and plumbing. Along with working on the engines that were mounted on frames and could be run within the training area, we learned to operate LCM's and LST's on the James River. The LCM, also known as a *Mike Boat* is the landing craft we have come to see often in war movies like *The Longest Day* and *Saving Private Ryan,* both depicting the Normandy Invasion in France on June 6[th,] 1944.

On one occasion, as we were being familiarized with the workings of the Mike Boat and during a smoke break, one soldier ground out his cigarette on the deck of the boat. A sergeant was on him in an instant, yelling at him, "This particular Mike Boat, now only used in training, landed at the famous Inchon landings commanded by General Douglas MacArthur during the Korean War,"! Why the soldier thought he could step on a cigarette butt on *any* Army vessel was a mystery to me. Well, at least we got a history lesson.

At Fort Eustis I met two guys from Texas who had bunks next to mine. Charlie Lawton was from Wichita Falls and Gene Gunn from Dallas. I used to kid them once we were allowed to wear civilian clothes while off duty, "Where are your cowboy boots and steer horn belt buckles?"

Charlie told me, "Most people in Texas don't dress like that." I replied, "Most people in the Bronx don't dress like that either."

Charlie and Gene had traveled to Fort Eustis together in Gene's red GTO, we traveled in that car whenever we had time off. We decided to visit Washington D.C. for Memorial Day 1966. We discussed whether or not we would wear uniforms and decided we should, in honor of those who had died protecting our country. Once in Washington we discovered that wearing the uniforms meant we would be saluting all day because there were officers everywhere you looked.

We visited the then temporary grave of John F. Kennedy. The eternal flame was surrounded by man-made grass and a white picket fence. As we were standing there a big black Cadillac with flags flying on the fenders pulled up. Out stepped the President of the United States, Lyndon Baines Johnson and the First Lady. They were quickly surrounded by Secret Service men in suits. The President laid a wreath next to the eternal flame and stood with bowed head and seemed to be saying a prayer. The Secret Service men were riveted on us. We should have saluted the Commander in Chief but were too dumbfounded to move, and the Secret Service men looked as if they would shoot us if we made a move. The President stayed for only a few minutes as people began to surround us. Later, reflecting on this extraordinary happenstance, we concluded that we should have saluted even though LBJ didn't look like he would have returned the salute. We were at first peeved that the Secret Service men kept checking us out. After all, we were soldiers in uniform and felt that, if anything went wrong we would protect our Commander in Chief. However, another incident enlightened us as to why the Secret Service would be so watchful of us.

We were approached by a short guy dressed in the uniform of the 82nd Airborne. He seemed a bit strange to me. I looked him over carefully but all seemed correct in terms of his uniform; the bloused jump boots, silver parachute wings, the shoulder patch of the 82nd and the paratrooper insignia on his garrison cap. But still something didn't seem right. We moved away from him as soon as we could. A while later we were approached and asked by a couple of MPs if we had seen such a guy. We asked, "What's the story with him?" The MPs told us, "The guy isn't even in the Army but likes to dress up as a paratrooper and strut around." So now we realized that dressing up in uniform might be a way for someone to get close enough to harm the President. That's why we were scrutinized by the Secret Service at JFK's gravesite.

President Johnson at John F. Kennedy Gravesite-Memorial Day 1966

As we walked around we kept hearing something that sounded like shotgun shells going off. We followed the sound and found ourselves at the Tomb of the Unknown Soldier. The gun like sounds came from the honor guard sentry as he clicked his heels together then marched back and forth. We paid close attention to his heels. Small steel "clickers" on the insides of the heels made a loud pop. It was a warm day and honor guards surrounded the memorial's walkways. Servicemen representing the five services--Army, Marines, Navy, Air Force, and Coast Guard kept repeating five after five, while standing at attention. Unfortunately, the heat got to one of them and he passed out, parting the bushes lining the walkway. The other guards did not move. However, there were medical personnel and a replacement guard at that guard post within minutes. We watched as President Johnson made an appearance and placed a wreath at the Tombs of the Unknown's. The crowd was silent and very respectful.

Afterward, we walked over to the Lincoln Memorial and then to the Washington Memorial. There was a long line for the elevator at the Washington Memorial so we hoofed it up the stairs to the top. It was a physically taxing climb but we were young soldiers and in good shape. Or so we all thought. Coming down, it was quite a bit easier.

Gene Gunn seemed like an old timer to us since he was twenty-six years old. He had been married and divorced and worked in an office in Dallas doing data processing. He had returned home on a pass driving along with Charlie Lawton. Just about everyone had gone home for a short stay. Upon our return we learned that Gunn never showed up to drive back to Fort Eustis. Charlie had Gene's phone number and called. He learned that Gene had tragically died in the "Lake O' Pines" in Texas. It was thought that he had suffered a heart attack while swimming and died from the heart attack, or perhaps drowned as a result of the attack. It especially drove the loss home when soldiers were sent to cut the locks off of his lockers and retrieve the contents to send home to his family. It looked and felt like the scenes we had all watched in dozens of movies where someone is killed and his buddies gather around as his personnel effects are gathered up by some unlucky guys tasked with performing this somber duty.

Gunn was a good guy and we would miss him. I recall on one occasion back at Fort Eustis, we were headed downtown in Gunn's car wearing civilian clothes and saw a young college age woman standing on the side of the road with travel bags, crying. Gene stopped and offered our help. She was trying to find a local school. We knew where it was and offered her a ride. She got in the car and said, "I'm happy to see you because there are so many soldiers around and I'm a bit afraid of them." She glanced up at the rear view mirror and saw behind it on the windshield a Fort Story parking permit. She looked at us and said, "You are soldiers aren't you." No question mark because it was more of a statement.

"Yes, we are" we said, and were very gentleman like, calmed her fears, and took her right to the school she was looking for. We did a good PR job for the Army and hopefully changed her thinking about soldiers.

One of the sergeants who trained us on diesel engines warned that, "A diesel engine could take off and run faster and faster until it destroyed itself."

He said, "At one point during our training this will happen" and added that, "Rather than control the situation you will all take off and run away." Well, we had a six-cylinder Gray Marine diesel engine that started revving higher and higher and, try as we might, we couldn't get the engine to slow down and stop. As predicted we all took off to get away from the engine before it blew, sending shrapnel all around. The sergeant stayed with the engine and calmly shut off the fuel supply. The engine slowed and stopped. He looked at us and said, "Now, why didn't you think of that?"

A more dangerous incident occurred while tuning the fuel injectors on a great big Enterprise engine. The bar was inserted into holes on the side of the flywheel and turned by hand to bring each piston up to its highest point in its stroke, one at a time. After doing this for each piston the order was given to start the engine. No one thought to remove the iron bar prior to hitting the start button. The flywheel spun and sent that iron bar crashing and ringing into the steel roof rafters before dropping down to the cement floor with a loud clang. If that bar had hit anyone, serious injury, or possibly death would have been the outcome. From that time on the engine would not be turned by the starter until it was checked to see that the bar was safely removed.

"T" school, as it was called, was not bad duty at all. We had nice barracks and actual toilets that flushed and with privacy partitions. But during my stay at Fort Eustis the word was getting around that someone came into the barracks late at night and sexually fondled people as they slept. I thought this was just another story that would turn out to be folklore. However, one night while sleeping I heard someone yell out loud, "Who the hell is touching my dick?" With that, someone ran right past me since I slept close to the door. It happened fast and no one was awake or quick enough to grab the guy.

Evidently, there were other soldiers who had experienced the same thing and it had been reported. One morning soon after yet another incident, the First Sergeant stood up on his elevated deck and said, "If you catch anybody doing this throw him out of the barracks window, no matter what floor you are on." I was struck by this because I felt that if anyone was caught and thrown out of a window the person who threw him would use as a defense that he was just following orders. There were over a hundred witnesses to that comment. Or was it an order? Anyway, it must have scared off the offender because it never happened again.

When Retreat was sounded at five-o-clock each evening everything halted and you were required to salute any flag visible or face where the bugle sounds might be coming from while outdoors. I found it comical, the lengths people would go to get indoors where you would not be required to salute or stand at attention. People would check their watches so they could plan their escape or they would scatter and run to the nearest building they could enter.

An interesting part of our training was firefighting school held at Portsmouth Naval Station in Virginia. We were ordered to report at a specific time to board a bus to the Navy base. We were told to wear our best starched uniforms and highly polished combat boots. There was a sergeant in charge of us for this training, and it wasn't lost on me that he was a paratrooper who would not allow any goofing around. Once on the bus he said, "At the end of the training there will be competition between us and the Navy sailors attending the same training." He added, "I've taken nineteen Army groups through this course, the Army beat the Navy each time and you will not be an exception."

At the Navy base, on our first day we attended classroom training where a crusty Navy Chief Petty Officer told us, "You will be fighting actual fires so it is imperative that you pay attention and follow orders."

We then were ordered by the Army sergeant, "Give me a column of twos outside to be marched to the mess hall, (galley in Naval terms), for your lunch break."

Once we began marching we got the order, "Double time." We double timed in step through a busy area. Clearly the paratrooper in charge wanted to put on a show for the sailors. They were impressed or just curious, many of them stopping to watch us pass by. Once we got to the galley we joined the sailors waiting in line. I was standing with my buddy, Charlie Lawton. Charlie had one hand in his pocket, which was not in keeping with uniform regulations. As our sergeant passed by Charlie he said in his best drill sergeant's voice, "Get your hand out of your pocket troop."

The sailors' expressions said, *I'm really glad I'm not a soldier.*

After the initial classroom instructions, we were given old uniforms to wear so as to not ruin ours and went out to the firefighting course. It was very impressive. It was made to look like a ship, just above weather deck with dogged hatches to enter various compartments. Once inside, the deck was like you might see over a draw-bridge, the kind that makes your tires hum. Below the deck was a pool of oil. We were trained on holding a fire hose the correct way to extinguish any type of fire and to hang on to the high pressure hose. A demonstration was made where a fire hose was chained to a vertical metal pipe about six feet from the ground, with a six-foot length of hose left loose down to the nozzle. The water was turned on and the hose went swinging wildly in all directions with that heavy brass nozzle cutting swaths through the air. There was no way to grab that nozzle; it could only be stopped by cutting off the water.

O.K., now to get the Navy guys pissed off. Six sailors were told to pick up the hose and hang on to it when the water was turned on. They held on for a few seconds and let it go. A dangerous thing to do. However, the Chief stood by the water source and cut it off at the first sign that they wouldn't be able to hold. Next, it was the Army's turn. The soldiers picked up the hose, got ready and dug their heels in. The water was turned on and the soldiers held. Mark up one for the Army.

The next exercise was to enter a burning compartment in the mock ship's structure and put out the fire. This time the hose was two inches in diameter rather than six. You had to first hose down the hot steel door, or hatch, as the sailors say, so you would be able to release the steel dogs, or what landlubbers would call levers, to unlock the door and enter. We entered an inferno, with flames coming up from the burning pool of oil below us. We worked the hose as instructed by the Chief who was with us the entire time, calling out orders and directions. The Chief Petty Officer and his assistants were on constant vigil seeing to it that no one was injured, and no one was.

The next thing we learned was how to use the equipment that created the foam that is used to smother a fire where water would not be the best choice. The apparatus was a gasoline-run pump with a hose sucking water from a small well and another hose inserted into a large can. The mixture of water and the substance in the can combined and created foam. Lots of it. We were told to make sure that the can we inserted the hose into was in fact the foam making stuff and not something that would make the fire worse, like oil or gasoline. The Chief told us, "You could always tell it was the right stuff because it smelled like a, "bucket full of assholes." Colorful Navy speak.

On the third and final day of training the competitive trials were to begin. We had three Navy teams and three Army teams. The first competition was to enter the burning room through the door or hatch that you hopefully had cooled down before touching. The hatch was opened and the Chief stood just inside it. He gave the order for us to move in while beating down the flames with the water as we had been trained to do. The Army guys instantly followed orders to move in to the burning room, to the point that the Chief had to grab them and hold them back.

The next contest was to see how fast the foam pump was put into operation. Each team had one person designated to give the orders to have his team correctly and quickly make foam. With both tests the Army was the winner in terms of the timed tests and the correct procedure used. I made an observation as to why the Army won hands down. It was due to the fact that the Army guys reacted instantly to orders while the sailors seemed to be hesitant.

Our paratrooper sergeant just beat the Navy with his twentieth consecutive win at what he called, "their own game."

We attended technical or "T" classes every day and the course was eight weeks. We studied quite a variety of topics such as diesel power, air conditioning, electric and refrigeration, all in preparation for being assigned to vessel maintenance. I was not too happy with having to work in a hot, noisy engine room but compared to what a lot of other soldiers had to do I didn't have any right to complain.

Chapter 11

On a warm day in June, 1966, we had graduation ceremonies. We all wore our summer class A uniforms which were our khakis. We had a soldier from the 82nd Airborne who had attended classes with us, as well as, one Green Beret Special Forces soldier. They were assigned to our classes in order to obtain an additional MOS, or Military Occupational Specialty to add to their Combat Arms MOS. Their regular units wanted to have some people trained to be able to help if technical circumstances arose.

I remember both soldiers well because we were all impressed with the famed Green Berets and the elite 82nd Airborne Division.

At this time, there was a new song on the radio we heard often called, the "Ballad of the Green Berets" sung by Sergeant Barry Saddler. I remember our sergeant challenging both of our classmates because they wore their jump boots bloused as airborne personnel do. The sergeant's claim was that since our technical school was not an Airborne unit they should dress like the rest of us. The paratrooper and the green beret stood their ground and both wore their Airborne class A, or dress uniforms, as they would normally have.

We had always heard that paratroopers didn't like us "straight legs," a name for soldiers not airborne and therefore held in disdain, but, these two were both great guys and treated us as equals. They knew they had our respect.

The paratrooper and the green beret both soon went back to their respective units and the rest of us were assigned to a unit deactivated after Korea that was presently being reactivated as the 165th Transportation Company Lighter Amphibious at Fort Story, Virginia Beach, Virginia. Soon after arrival at the 165th I learned that since they had already assigned enough guys to the maintenance platoon, all of us late arrivals would be trained as drivers of the Lighter Amphibious Resupply Cargo Five Ton "LARC." This was great news to me and my friend, Joe Callahan. We would rather be driving them as opposed to fixing them.

The LARC is thirty-five feet long, ten-feet wide and eleven-feet high. It is powered by a powerful V-8 Cummins diesel engine. It could do approximately 35 MPH on land and 12 Knots on water. The LARC is made of aluminum and left silver in color rather than painting it olive drab as most military vehicles are. It is shaped like a boat hull except for the five-foot-high tires that are low pressure and wide, enabling it to move on sand quite well. On the tire is written, "Super Sand Floatation." It can be driven in two-

Costner and Callahan

61

wheel or four-wheel drive. The traction was always so good that I rarely, if ever, used four-wheel drive.

The LARC is a vehicle that is part truck and part boat. It has four wheels, a steering wheel, and a rudder. There are several levers for changing from land mode into boat mode. As you can see in the picture, there is a small cabin for the operator but most of the vehicle is devoted to carrying cargo. (You can also see in the picture on page sixty-one that Joe's boots are not bloused as was often the case, no matter how many times Sergeant Taffe admonished him). You can see the other soldier's boots are bloused as per regulations. The primary role we played was off-loading ships full of supplies, bloused boots or not, as Joe saw it.

We began training on the LARC V or LARC, as we typically called it, by piling onto the decks of several vehicles and taking turns driving it through trails in the woods at Fort Story, near Virginia Beach, Virginia. There were sergeant instructors with us at all times. Because there were about thirty guys on each LARC we didn't drive as much as ride on the deck, trying not to get bounced off since there were no sides to the cargo deck. There was no suspension, only the bounce from the large low pressure tires. It was hot and dusty but kind of fun. One young sergeant ordered all of us off the vehicle as he attempted to drive up a very steep incline. Each try had the LARC bouncing like crazy and looking like it was going to pitch-pole over and crash. He finally made it after about four attempts; it was very impressive that this vehicle, the size of a bus, could climb that hill.

There were three seats across the cab, with the driver's seat in the middle. Most often we would drive standing up with our head and part of our shoulders above the windshield, leaning on the top of it for support. Since the LARC had only two speeds, high and low, it is only shifted when it was completely stopped. With power steering and brakes you could easily drive it with just your left foot on the accelerator and left hand on the steering wheel while on land or in the water.

After training on land for weeks it was time to try and drive the LARC off a beach and into the water, the water being Chesapeake Bay in Virginia. At first we learned to approach the beach, turn off the cooling fan, move forward, and engage marine drive. Now you were a boat. We drove around in the water in a great arc and then headed back to the beach, sometimes followed by friendly dolphins. To get back on land you approached the beach, engaged land drive once you felt your wheels were on the bottom, disengaged marine drive and moved up until you were completely out of the water. Now you let the fan area in the rear of the LARC drain for a minute and empty before turning the cooling fan back on so as not to blow water all around the engine compartment. While in the water the fan remained disengaged while cooling was taken over by a heat exchange system in the rear and on the bottom of the LARC.

While in the water we were a boat or a vessel, as the Army said. Interesting side note: while in class we were told it was hard to make the distinction between what is a boat or a ship so the Army calls all water craft, "vessels." We also learned that the Army has more total vessels than does the Navy.

Anyhow, operating a vessel is a little different than driving a land vehicle. Which we found out soon enough when we were given the task of taking on a load of fake cargo from a ship. The driver would have to get alongside the ship and hold a position below the crane's cable so the cargo could be lowered for a stevedore to jockey it into place and have the cargo dropped on to your deck. The first thing you had to do was get to the ship and maneuver your LARC into place. The first guy to try it approached the side of the ship, forgot that in the water, applying the foot brakes has no effect and slammed into the ship. To slow or stop you had to reverse the prop. Some guys riding on the deck got knocked down, fortunately there were no injuries.

With practice, we came to be fairly good at operating the LARC on land or sea. The training kept to regular hours so we spent a lot of time on the Virginia Beach strip drinking what we called "near beer" because it was a reduced alcohol content beer, and trying to pick up girls with not much success.

One girl in particular I didn't have much success with was the proverbial girl back home. I met her the summer my family moved to Patchogue, Long Island in 1962. Jean was one of the four or five neighborhood girls who were in our local group and attended Patchogue High School. I was immediately attracted to her. Jean was slender and pretty with platinum hair and was more mature than most girls her age. Jean was always working somewhere in town and did so without even having a car to get around. Whenever I knew where she was working I would make it a point to do business with that store, without taking too much of her time so she wouldn't get in trouble with her boss. At one time, she was working in a bank and the male employees kept hovering around her so she was fired instead of them. That's how it was back in 1965; employers could get away with that kind of stuff.

Anyway, she did give me her telephone number and I would call her from time to time. We often talked for an hour. I asked her out on several occasions; but she always declined but was very nice about it. I always told her, "You're saving me up for a rainy day." It was always a good day when I would see her walking the halls at school. I would fall in with her and walk her to her class even if it made me late for mine. I felt that she liked me and the attention I gave her but she never let me get any closer. The guy she was dating at one point was a cousin of one of my friends. He always said his cousin was a jerk and he didn't know what she saw in him.

Neither did I.

The time after graduation went quickly and I rarely saw her. She and I were both working. I did see her once walking home while I was driving my employer's sign truck through town. I stopped, said hello, and offered her a ride She climbed into the truck, and while I made a U-turn I remember shaking so bad I could hardly depress the clutch, (Come on, it was a stiff clutch) and hoping she wouldn't notice. I called her a couple of times from Fort Story, Virginia and when I had a three-day pass coming I called, asking if I could see her. She said she took the train each morning very early to attend school in Queens, New York and didn't get home until late. Since my pass didn't include any weekend days it seemed I wouldn't get a chance to see her. So, I decided that I would take her train and spend the hour long train ride to Queens with her.

I arranged for a taxi to pick me up at my home and take me to the Patchogue train station. The driver happened to be a police officer I knew, and he was late. The cop sped to the train station and I got there just before the train left and before I could buy a ticket. The cop/taxi driver told me there was no charge for the taxi and to just jump on the train and buy a ticket from the conductor. I started my way through the empty rear cars toward the front. I met up with the conductor who took a ticket and did his punching thing and handed it to me. As I started to get my wallet out he said, "No charge, I was in the Army too." I was in uniform, thinking it might help with the object of my affection. It didn't.

A phrase heard very often in the military at the time covering any mishap or setback was, "Sorry 'bout that." It applied here. So far the uniform got me a free taxi ride and a free train ticket, round trip. I met Jean in the coffee car. We sat and drank coffee and talked while the train rumbled on to Queens. I should have thought of something dramatic like the movie in where the couple arrange to meet on the observation deck of the Empire State Building upon the soldier's returning to New York. To me it was a kind of romantic moment. The young soldier leaving for the war, maybe never to return, says goodbye to the beautiful platinum blonde.

Ah, the movies, they'll kill ya'.

Back at Fort Story we found ourselves being ordered to do some infantry-like field training using blanks in our rifles. We dug foxholes along a dirt road and hunkered down in them, taking shifts standing guard while one of us slept. Clarkson, the guy I had as a foxhole partner was from Washington State where his parents ran a hops farm. They provided hops for Olympia Beer. While it was my watch at night three aggressors across the road were sneaking through a tree line, I opened up on them with my M-14 rifle. They kept running. There was no procedure to ensure they didn't just get back in the game without a scorer making the observation. However, I knew I had gotten them all.

During this same exercise we walked through swamps. The water was only a foot deep but covered in small green buds. With every step you took the buds parted and you could see the brown water. What was really of concern was the occasional snake I saw gliding across the top of the water. I was sure they were water moccasins or cotton mouths as they are called. A sergeant confirmed this for me. While we trained there was a group of marines using the area too. We came upon one Marine floating on top of a log in a small pond. Our sergeant told the marine, "There are snakes around and I don't think your position on that log is a safe choice."

While doing the field exercises our M-14 rifles needed to have blank adapters fixed to the rifle or they would not fire semi-automatic. Without an actual bullet moving down the barrel, not enough gas pressure built up to throw back the bolt and chamber another round. The blank adapter was a simple metal device attached to the rifle by the bayonet mount. A short and small circumference tube fit down into the rifle barrel and offered enough resistance to the escaping gas to operate the semi-automatic function. The adapters worked well, but one guy named Dom managed to have the muzzle of his rifle blown open, looking like a peeled banana. No problem, they just got him another rifle; the Army had lots of them.

As we cleaned up all our field gear I had a problem getting my rifle cleared for return to the armory. I cleaned it and presented it to the armorer three times and he rejected it as dirty each time. I was pissed. I knew the rifle was as clean as it was going to get. To prove it I stood it up against a wall and didn't touch it. After a short while I brought it back up to the armorer; he checked it over and declared it clean and placed it in the rifle rack. What bullshit, the Army can really jerk you around at times. My day wasn't getting any better. I spent so much time on the rifle that I couldn't get my field gear cleaned and displayed on my bunk in time for an inspection by Lieutenant Doran. Just before the Lieutenant arrived I had a fit and threw all my stuff around the barracks. Helmet went one way, mess kit another, pack yet another and so it went.

Lieutenant Doran arrived and started his inspection. I didn't know what to expect. When he got to my bunk and saw that the field gear was not displayed "by the book" he looked around saw my stuff strewn all over. He asked, "What happened here, Capainolo?" I told him, "My rifle was dirtied firing blanks and I had to present it to the armorer four times before it passed inspection." I said. "I ran out of time to clean my gear so I had a shit fit, sir."

The Lieutenant told me, "get your stuff together and cleaned. I'll be back to inspect again in ten minutes." Even that was too short a time to get done but as soon as he left my buddies all pitched in and got me inspection ready. Lieutenant Doran came back; he passed me on the inspection. I'm pretty sure he held back a smile when I gave him my "shit fit" explanation. Lieutenant Doran was an excellent officer who was well respected and liked by his platoon. His favorite admonishment was "knock off the bullshit" said in his Virginia accent.

An event that was of some interest occurred while at Fort Story. I saw a LARC parked on an asphalt lot with people using reflective panels to light the LARC for a movie being filmed that was to be a training film. The LARC was somewhat taken apart to provide access to the interior for the camera. The actor playing the part of the driver (who would be one of us in the real world) was an enlisted soldier named Johnny Crawford. He had played the son of *The Rifleman* on the TV show of the same name. *The Rifleman* character was played by an ex-pro baseball player named Chuck Connors.

There was another Lieutenant in the 165th who was not a platoon leader but just seemed to work on administrative duties. He was very effeminate and I guessed homosexual. On the same day as the field gear cleaning and inspections he happened to be standing on the second floor landing of my barracks. As I got up to the landing and was standing face to face with him he looked at me and said, in an attempt at a sexy low growl, "Pasquale." Nobody in the Army called each other by their first name, especially if it's Pasquale, so he must have looked it up. Being from Long Island and just a boat ride across the Great South Bay from famous gay communities, Cherry Grove and the Fire Island Pines, I was not unnerved. He never made any advances and I had no problem with his being gay. Soon after, he was reassigned to another unit so he never shipped out with us to Vietnam. Of course this was a long time before "don't ask, don't tell", maybe he left the Army.

Soon came the orders for the 165th to go to Vietnam. It was no surprise to us since we all expected it. However, two men had their own shit fit over the news and had to be restrained and taken away in an ambulance. I never heard what had become of them since we left shortly after and they did not ship out with us. All we needed was a way to get there. In order to move out quickly we started living out of our duffle bags. I was surprised but happy to learn that since we weren't doing anything we were all given a three-day pass. Charlie Lawton lived in Wichita Falls, Texas and decided not to go home because most of the time would be spent traveling. I asked him if he wanted to go to New York with me and get to see the city.

He readily agreed. We teamed up with a guy named Shindler who lived in New Jersey just across the Hudson River from Manhattan. We drove to New York City in his car and he dropped us off by the bus terminal on Eighth Avenue. I called my father who talked me into going up to Yonkers to see my Aunt Mary. He said, "I'll pick you up in the old Bronx neighborhood after work at the St. Lawrence subway stop." It was close to the Bronx River Parkway that would take us up to Yonkers."

So with time to kill, we went into a Chock Full of Nuts coffee shop just across from the bus station. That's where Charlie got his first dose of New York City. The counter guy kept bussing the dirty dishes and utensils and didn't look up to take our order. I just said what I wanted knowing he would hear me. Charlie was waiting for him or someone to look up and ask what he would like. After a time, I told Charlie to, "just say what you want." With that Charlie asked for a "hot butterscotch sundae, or some such thing." The counter guy now looked up at Charlie and said, "What the hell is that, some new dance or something?" Charlie sheepishly amended his order.

Once we left the café we walked around looking at the shops and the people rushing around then went down to the subway station to head up to the Bronx. Rush hour had started, there was the typical crowd running for their trains. We were in no particular hurry and Charlie, being about six feet two, was taking big, long but slow steps. I saw, with my peripheral vision, a short guy in business attire carrying a briefcase trying desperately to get around Charlie. The guy blurted out, "Get the fuck out of the way, will 'ya, buddy?" So far, Charlie was getting the whole New York rudeness treatment.

We boarded the Pelham Bay line subway and took it up to the Bronx. We were underground until we came up and on to the elevated subway at Hunts Point. Charlie looked out the windows and said, "I can hardly believe it,"

I said, "Believe what?"

He said, "Since we've been hurtling through the subway tunnel for a half-hour I expected to be out of the city and I'm amazed that we aren't."

It's a big city.

We still had more time to kill so after getting off the subway at St. Lawrence Avenue we were about to go to the local candy store where everyone meets, and I met and said hello to Carol Beaumonte who had been part of my Bronx group of friends. Once at the candy store Charlie got to meet other friends who, to him, looked and sounded like a bunch of gangsters. At the prearranged time we met up with my father and rode up to my Aunt Mary's house. She was thrilled with Charlie's Texas accent.

The next day we met with Lenny Cook and took Charlie up the Empire State Building. It was comical to see how he put his hand on the wall to steady himself and peered down to get a look. All and all it was a great trip for Charlie from Texas. When we got back to Fort Story he had stories to tell and told everyone he felt like he had been in "West Side Story."

After returning to Fort Story we got orders to transport our LARCs to Norfolk Naval Station where they would be loaded onto a ship and sent to Vietnam. We lined up about half of our total LARCVs and traveled in a convoy through the regular civilian roads. We drove from Fort Story in Virginia Beach to Portsmouth Naval Base, Virginia, turning many civilian heads that had never seen this big boat with wheels and certainly not on regular highways. Only half of our LARCs made this first trip because it was all that our particular assigned naval vessel could carry. It was great fun.

Soon after, we were to board a ship at Oakland Army Terminal for transport to Vietnam. We had to move quickly to get to the ship, so we would be traveling in groups of about forty people, utilizing various airlines and wearing our field gear: helmets, packs, web pistol belts, ammunition pouches, and M-14 rifles. My group was the first to go. We were bussed to Richmond to board our first flight west. The rifles were a problem at every airliner we were to board. The pilots would not let us on board with them. After a short delay an Army staff car pulled up, and within minutes, we began boarding. The pilot stood in the doorway of the plane and inspected our rifles to ensure there were no bullets in the receiver. This was done in order to be safe and prevent any unintended discharge. I boarded the plane never having flown before and thought it was great. Our trip took us from Richmond, Virginia, to Atlanta, Georgia, Dallas, Texas, and finally to San Francisco.

While in the various airports we were quite an unusual sight. We actually stacked arms. That is where three refiles are made into a triangle and they stand by themselves. We posted a guard and answered many questions the civilians had like, "What kind of a gun is that?" And, "Where are you guys going?" The little boys in particular were fascinated by seeing all the soldiers and the rifles. On one of the flights when the flight attendant, called stewardesses then, went past with the beverage cart I felt it just touch the butt of my rifle. The stewardess leaned over me and asked, "Could you just move your *gun* out of the aisle?"

I looked at Joe Callahan and chuckled, since anybody having been in the military knows the old saying. While grabbing their crotch in one hand and holding their rifle in the other; "This is my weapon, this is my gun, this is for fighting, this is for fun." In the military you never refer to your weapon as a gun. This was a short phrase to remember that.

A few minutes later the stewardess returned, smiling, and said, "I meant your weapon; I have a brother in the Marines."

At each airport we boarded the plane after all the civilians were on and seated. We came through the rear door rather than the sides. As we were throwing down all of our gear, trying to make room for ourselves, a man in a business suit stowed his briefcase in the overhead and turned to look at us. He asked, "Where are you guys going?" Of course he got the answer, "Vietnam." With that he jumped up, got his briefcase down and started down the aisle. A stewardess stopped him and asked what the problem was. He said he must be on the wrong plane "Cause these guys are going to Vietnam."

The stewardess explained to him that, "The plane will be landing in San Francisco and the soldiers will be moving on to other transportation."

Chapter 12

It was night by the time we got to Oakland Army Terminal. We got off the bus and were directed to a doorway in what looked like a big black wall. It was in fact the side of an enormous ship, the "General Edwin D. Patrick". We were directed to the sleeping quarters we would occupy for the next twenty-one days crossing the Pacific Ocean. Each of us was issued two short lengths of twine that was used to hang our rifles from the bottom of the cot above. For the whole trip we had rifles swinging with the rolling of the ship at about six inches above our noses and smelling like gun oil. I say cot but it was more like canvas stretched between metal pipes sort of like a trampoline and it had four tiers.

The next morning there was a Fifth Army band playing for our sendoff. On the pier there were quite a few civilians, no doubt families of those close enough or determined enough to make the trip from their hometowns to say goodbye.

Once untied, the ship started to move and was being attended to by several tugboats. As we were leaving the bay we passed under a bridge. I can never remember which bridge is which, the Oakland Bay Bridge or the Golden Gate. People on foot lined the whole bridge. They were throwing pennies down on us as we passed underneath. It was some kind of war protest but the reason for the pennies was lost to us. The tugboats stayed alongside us for some distance, blowing their horns with men waving from their decks, wishing us good luck. I will never forget those guys.

So we were on our way. Being from Long Island and having had experience with boats I didn't think sea sickness would be a problem. Guess again. I lay on my canvas cot looking around, and was amazed to see the prone bodies of the troops rising and falling with the motion of the ship. I got seasick on the first night out. I made it to the "head" as the sailors call the toilet, the "latrine" in Army parlance. I threw up only once on the first night but felt woozy, with my head spinning, for the next five days. Finally, I got my sea legs and was O.K. for the rest of the twenty-one-day trip. Some guys were so bad they were placed in the ship's sickbay, mostly due to dehydration from the constant vomiting. Dramamine pills were available at the water fountains but they didn't seem to help much. On about the third day out we found ourselves in a storm. Guards were posted to keep everyone off the weather deck because there was a danger they could be swept overboard. Eating in the galley was a challenge. As the ship rolled, trays would slide down the table and everyone would have his buddy's food in front of him. Looking out a porthole you would see sky one minute and nothing but water the next. We felt a consistent shuddering of the ship and asked a sailor what it was. He said, "That's when the propeller comes out of the water." Great.

When the storm passed and we were allowed on deck we could see lots of flying fish coming out of the water by the bow. One curious soldier asked a sailor if there were sharks around here. He said, "Are you kidding? This is the South China Sea. Ten men couldn't throw me off this ship; the sharks would have you before you hit the water." Oh well, we weren't going swimming anyway.

The weather was getting warm as we approached the Equator. We didn't know the significance of that but would soon find out. It seems the Navy has an initiation for all military personnel crossing the Equator for the first time. We were ordered to strip down to our drawers and shower shoes then run through a gauntlet of about fifty guys slapping us on our buttocks with shower flip flops. Some kind of hot cinnamon was put in our mouths, with the same Q Tip used over and over. There was a tunnel made of canvas with scrapings from food trays thrown in and made real soggy and disgusting wetted down with fire hoses. We crawled through this tunnel on hands and knees, getting sprayed continuously with fire hoses. The grand finale was a large fat sergeant with a trident and a crown billed as King Neptune reclining on a chaise lounge. His belly was smeared with Crisco lard and we had to kiss his belly. Ugh!

But, the Army struck back. Just over the reclining King Neptune there was a walkway that traversed the ship port and starboard. Right and left to landlubbers. Several wastepaper baskets were filled with water, and from this walkway the water was dumped on King Neptune. The water was dumped accurately by members of the 11th Artillery. We heard sometime later that the 11th Artillery's fire base was overrun by the enemy. This, of course, was another rumor that was not substantiated and I hope was not true.

Our first stop off the coast of Vietnam was in the Southern portion at a place called Vung Tau. As we approached, we had a US Navy warship escort. Our ship and the warship signaled each other with the light they use for that purpose. We, of course, couldn't decipher the signal but the whole escort thing was exciting.

The 11th Artillery went ashore the first day, and we stayed aboard as night settled in. We would depart in the morning to cruise up the coast to Cam Ranh Bay. The ship we were on was not only for carrying troops and was not unlike an ocean liner. Above decks things were very different from our experience thus far. The ship was also used for carrying U.S. dependents, although not to a combat zone, which all of Vietnam was. There were shops and a dining area complete with tablecloths and white jacketed stewards. Since we were the only military aboard left for the remainder of the voyage we were invited to come up and dine in the dining room. The tables each had four places, were covered in white tablecloths and were served by the stewards. So this was how the other half lived. We had dinner that night and breakfast the next morning prior to stopping at Cam Ranh Bay.

Chapter 13

In order to get us ashore a landing craft came up alongside the ship. Duffel bags were slid down a chute onto the LCM landing craft or "Mike Boat". We went aboard through an open port just about level with the LCM and headed for shore. Since most things are done in the Army in alphabetical order, I was aboard the first boat along with our captain and his staff. As the Mike Boat nudged up to shore the ramp went down and we were given the order, "Forward March." Happily, there was no firing and none had been expected since Cam Ranh Bay was a very secure area. Each Army unit has a flag that identifies it called a "guide on." It is fastened to a long flag staff. Ours would identify us as the 165th Transportation Company. Most orders in marching or what is known as close order drill is called out in two parts, as in forward march. As the first part of the order is called, the guide on bearer raises the flag snappily and brings it down just as snappy when the second part of the order is given.

Since I was in the first group to come ashore I saw the guide on being planted in the soil of South Vietnam. A tiny bit of history was made and it was exciting.

A line of trucks was waiting to take us to our Company area. When we got there we saw nothing but sand. Nothing was prepared for us. The area was staked out and we began erecting our eight man GP tents. Besides putting up the tents we had to build walls of sandbags around the tent. It was a lot of work and kept us busy around the clock. A first there were no showers or mess hall, but luckily latrines were made available quickly. I found the Army to be very good at protecting soldiers' health with good hygiene and with all of the inoculations we had to endure.

Since our vehicles had not arrived we worked at making our Company area livable. Thankfully we had a guy named Smith who we called "Smitty" who was a carpenter and a godsend. He had a mess hall built in short order and, throughout our oversees experience, he built many welcomed additions like tent frames, showers, cat walks and even a basketball court. He was eventually promoted to sergeant and it was well deserved.

Thank you, Smitty.

Arriving at Cam Ranh Bay just in time to see the Bob Hope Christmas show was a treat for us. It was held at South Beach, (named way before the TV show) we sat on a sand hill along with thousands of other soldiers, some Air Force people, and some guys from the base hospital recovering from wounds or illness. They wore their hospital gowns; many of them in wheel chairs, and they were given access to the front row. Some guys from the Signal Corps. climbed utility poles and got bird's eye views.

Looking into the background of the picture on page sixty-one taken at Cam Ranh Bay you see a plywood partition. Within the partition there was a six-inch pipe sticking out of the ground that allowed some privacy for soldiers to urinate. While sitting on a sand hill with a couple thousand other soldiers waiting for Joey Heatherton to arrive, an Air Force guy sitting next to me who was not familiar with the Army's area asked, "Where can I go to take a pee?" I pointed out one of these rudimentarily urinals and he kind of looked at me in disbelief. He went and when he returned he had a story for some of his airman buddies. He looked at me and said, "You Army guys sure got it rough".

I replied, "You don't know the half of it, peeing in a pipe is no big deal."

Real soldiers don't need porcelain.

Bob Hope and the rest of the show people were great. Joey Heatherton sang and danced and Anita Bryant had everyone in tears singing "White Christmas" with the troops. We loved Bob Hope and he was highly respected for the tours he made to combat areas beginning in World War II and continuing through Korea, Vietnam and beyond. Bob would always say the service people at these shows were the greatest audiences in the world.

Half of our vehicles arrived and the other half was taking a different route around Africa. Again, since everything is in alphabetical order and my name beginning with C, I was selected to be one of the first LARCs to start lightering operations. It was exciting and also scary. We were about to start doing what we had been trained to do, amphibious lightering. Bringing in all manner of cargo and thus participate in the war effort.

The ships were anchored farther out than the one we had in training. Adding to this, my radio was not working, so Lieutenant Doran assigned another LARC to stay with me as a buddy LARC. When we got to shipside we found another LARC company operating and who were experienced. We found out real soon that there was competition in getting a load of cargo and they were not letting the new guys in. Being new, with limited experience, I found that I was not aggressive enough but I would quickly learn. We worked twelve hours a day, seven days a week so I got plenty of immediate practice. Driving a LARC was not difficult and it was a trustworthy machine on land and sea. I can't recall ever seeing or hearing of a LARC that got stuck. The wheels were large and soft, and the vehicle could be operated in two-wheel or four-wheel drive.

The hardest part of operating a LARC was to keep it steady alongside the ship directly under where the boom cable would lower its cargo. The crane operator aboard ship could not see the LARC in the water below so he relied on hand signals from a soldier looking over the edge of the ship's deck. Stevedores had the unenviable job of grabbing hold of the cargo and muscling it into place, yelling "drop it!" when it was in position. Simple enough? Not really, when you consider the LARC is tossing around in the waves and the load on the end of the cable from the ship was often swinging around. It was dangerous work for stevedores who could be crushed between the load and the hull of a ship.

Napalm bombs were particularly troublesome because they were longer than the LARC's deck was wide and therefore extended out about eighteen inches off each side. I once had a stevedore who had a napalm bomb that got away from him. It was swinging around and tipping front to rear. I held my LARC under him for as long as I could. He was in danger of being pinned between the bomb and the ship and everyone was yelling, "Let go! Just drop into the water." He just wouldn't do it. Once your LARC got about three feet away from the ship all you could do was circle around and come in for another try. I got under him and he let go and dropped onto my deck.

I asked him, "Why the hell wouldn't you let go?"

He said, "I'm afraid of the sharks and I can't swim."

There were three or four LARCs all around and he would have been pulled out of the water immediately.

During an anti-speeding campaign one of our LARCs was heading out to the Air Force ammunition dump at the incredible speed of thirty-five miles per hour in a thirty mile an hour posted speed zone. He was on a causeway with beach and water on both sides. He was pursued by two MP's in a jeep. He crossed over the beach, entered the water, engaged marine drive and waved goodbye to the MPs.

Being amphibious has many advantages.

A few weeks later the rest of our vehicles arrived. A Sergeant Jerel had escorted the vehicles and he met us at the beach motor pool just in time to return to the Company area at the end of our day shift at 6:00 PM. As I boarded the LARC with about twenty-five other guys and took a seat on the deck I noticed a lot of guys checking their watches. At first I didn't know why, and then I realized that at

6:00 PM each night there was a big controlled explosion managed by the engineers. They would blow up a portion of a big hill near the motor pool to get material needed to make concrete. There was nothing but sand where we were but I learned that you can't make concrete with beach sand. So the explosion took place right on time and scared the hell out of Sergeant Jerel. He ducked and reached for his .45 cal. pistol. He looked around at us trying to understand why we took no action and looked as if nothing happened. He soon figured out he had been had.

We could have warned him, but what fun would that be?

Joe Callahan

Vietnamese stevedores positioning 750 lb. bombs onto a LARC's deck

Getting in tight to transfer a stevedore

Joe Callahan ready to deliver bombs to the Air Force

Pat Capainolo, left & Joe Callahan right

LARC coming ashore

Machine gun we thankfully didn't have occasion to use

George Wilson, from England, never had so much fun!

Joe Callahan with LARC 198

Water Buffalo, didn't like Callahan much

LARC V Cab and Instrument panel

Pat Capainolo, traded in a LARC for a Jeep

Pat Capainolo, 2nd. Platoon Jeep driver, call letters 2 Delta

My good Friend Charlie Lawton with LIP (Local Indigenous Personnel)

Bates wielding the infamous machete, cutting down coconuts

Of course the rifle wasn't loaded. The GI on the left is Bob Bellor

LARC under weigh

Just a few of our LARC s

Jeep with mounted machine gun protecting us at Tan Son Nuht Airport, Saigon

Temples or Wats, Bangkok., Thailand

Pat Capainolo at the Temple of the Golden Buddha, Bangkok., Thailand

Temple in Bangkok., Thailand

Chapter 14

We soon got up to speed with operations and moved some three hundred or so tons of cargo each shift. That would equate to sixty runs out to a ship, coming ashore, and bringing the cargo to its designated destination, usually Army or Air Force. We carried seven hundred and fifty pound bombs, five hundred pound bombs, napalm bombs, as well as the fins and detonators for those bombs. These were assembled by Air Force personnel.

One night I had a load of small wood boxes, each with a padlock. There were a few pallets of these with banding material holding them tightly. As I traveled along some very badly rutted roads the load bounced considerably. Some of the banding material snapped and about a dozen of these small boxes bounced off my deck landing in the roadway. I stopped, jumped down and gathered up the boxes, tossing them back up onto the deck. I then continued on to the Air Force dump.

There was an Air Force guard posted at the entrance and when he saw the loose boxes he asked, "What happened?"

I told him, "Some banding broke and boxes fell off the LARC onto the road."

He got kind of nervous, got on his field phone and called for the bomb disposal unit.

I asked him, "What's going on?"

He said, "Those boxes contain bomb fuses and they have to be handled very carefully or they could explode, setting off a chain reaction. We would be vaporized."

When the bomb disposal people got there they picked up the loose boxes like they contained nitro or something and put them into a truck. They got a forklift to gently pick up the remaining pallets that were safely banded.

You know, it would have been nice to get some kind of safety tip.

We were very fortunate not to have been in combat, but we did lose people to accidents. I had the occasion to pick up a pallet of perforated steel plating. These are sections of steel plating that link together to form a surface that could be used for a runway for airplanes. The plating is so heavy we just carried one pallet at a time. When I got to the Air Force dump the forklift they had couldn't begin to pick up the load. So I was asked to, "drive over to where that crane is and get under the cable hanging down." I did so and we got the hook at the bottom of the cable and secured it to the load. As a civilian working at a sign company I had worked with a crane, lifting neon signs, and I knew that as soon as the load was lifted off of the deck it would swing one way or another to get plumb. Behind the driver of the LARC there was a very thick wall of aluminum about three feet high to protect the driver from a shifting load. I was safely behind it but the airman was standing on the cargo side of the wall leaning on it. I warned him, "We can't tell which way the load is going to swing and if it comes your way you could be pinned." He said he'd be O.K. and gave the crane operator the thumbs up signal to lift the load.

Sure enough, as I had feared, the load headed right for the airman and he was about to get squashed. He did the only thing he could do; he dove off of the LARC, landing on some of that same plating comprising the surface we were on. Not a soft landing, I heard the crash of the load against my wall of protection and heard the airman go splat on the deck below. I jumped down to check him out. I didn't see any injury except that he was out cold. The crane operator called for an ambulance that arrived shortly and took the injured man away, still unconscious. I never heard anything more about it; I hope he was O.K.

Our Company area consisted of eight-man tents with a three-foot wall of sandbags all around except for the entrance ways on either side of the tent. We each made our own personal space to our liking, using scrap lumber, called "dunnage" that was originally used in a ship's hold to keep the cargo from shifting around. The Army hired Vietnamese women to do the laundry and clean the tents, make up bunks, etc. They did a good job and we were happy to have them.

One of our guys happened to be traveling along a familiar road and saw a group of Vietnamese attending to a woman who had collapsed. He stopped to see if he could help but the woman was unconscious. After a few minutes he decided to pick her up and bring her to the Army medical facilities. The woman was examined and it was determined that she had the bubonic plague. This is the same plague that devastated Europe, killing many thousands of people during the 12th Century. We had already been vaccinated for it back "stateside".

Our guy was made to remove all of his clothing and get a booster shot as a supplement to the plague vaccination we had all previously received. The truck he transported her in was eventually taken into a large field and scorched with a flame thrower. The tires, canvas roof and seats were all burned away. If I hadn't seen it with my own eyes I wouldn't have thought it possible, but a couple of months later we got the truck back all restored and ready for duty. There is very little on an Army truck that is flammable.

Soldiers came around to each tent and sprayed a white powder into the sand bags to kill any fleas present. We were told the fleas spread the plague and they were transported around by rats. My mother saw a news report that plague had broken out at the large military complex at Cam Ranh Bay, Vietnam. She knew it was where I was and called our family doctor to ask questions about the plague. He told her not to worry since he knew we all had been vaccinated for plague and were being given booster shots. He told her the Army was very good at managing things like this and assured her that I was in good hands. I later found out that he had done his military service as an Army doctor. We had heard that there were some fatalities among the Vietnamese and that six soldiers had contracted the disease, all six recovered.

We had a corporal named Levear who carried himself like a tough guy and a lot of people thought he was someone not to be trifled with. He was from a tough neighborhood in Brooklyn, either Brownsville or Bedford Stuyvesant. One night, as we were off duty, my tent buddies and I were listening to music, playing cards and drinking beer. We could hear in the distance the booming sound of either artillery or mortars and the tent sides were moving with the concussions. It got our attention but we dismissed it as out-going rather than in-coming. Someone yelled, "Hey Levear, you're pissing in your bunk." Since his cot was next to mine I looked and sure enough the piss was running down his leg and pooling on the floor.

That pretty much ended his tough guy persona.

Another tough guy, one of maintenance platoon's mechanics, decided he wanted to take a ride on one of the LARCs. Since there were so many of us operating ship to shore, about thirty as I recall, he hitched on to the first LARC leaving the beach and heading out to a ship. The water was rough that day with three foot waves and water washing over the cargo deck. The LARC's cargo deck was only inches out of the water to make loading and unloading easier than having to go over sides or gunwales, in marine terms.

Water rushing over the deck was normal and of no concern, except to him. He was so scared he started screaming to be taken back to the beach. Turning around without picking up a load was unheard of except for a dire emergency, and his being scared was not. Screaming did him no good, so he started threatening, which did even less, since he started whining like an eleven-year old girl. Finally, one of the LARC's, loaded and heading back to the beach, came alongside in response to a radio communicated request. I was already alongside but was heading out and only stopped to render whatever assistance I could. The tough guy was backed up against the engine compartment and was hanging on to a hand rail for dear life. We tried to talk him into letting go and making a six-inch jump on to the LARC that would take him back to the beach. We could barely pry his fingers off the handrail. I can't remember ever seeing anyone so terrified. We finally had to put one soldier on each side of him and shove him forcibly onto the deck of the LARC that would return him to the beach. No one took his tough guy stance seriously again.

I can understand someone being afraid but some exhibited it with a lot more dignity. We had a soldier who came from California and looked like a golden California athlete or surfer. His name was John Gageiano and he was a Golden Gloves boxer and a great guy. I once put the gloves on and boxed with him. I tried and tried to hit him until my arms felt like they were a ton each. He just kept covering up and being defensive. He no doubt could have creamed me anytime but didn't even give me a tap.

Somebody got the idea that Gageiano should box Sergeant Thatcher from the first platoon. The match was set and it took place in a square where the wood catwalks came together, making an area about twelve by twelve feet. It was built about four to six inches above the ground. The fight started and the two of them boxed with some skill. No one was landing any great punches, but Sergeant Thatcher got frustrated and started swinging for the moon. The more he couldn't hit Gageiano, the more frustrated he became. It was a battle between an enlisted man and an NCO, so there was considerable interest and a sizeable crowd watching.

At one point during the match Gageiano went too far back and stepped off the catwalk. He started hopping around and limping because he had turned his ankle. That ended the boxing match. The next day I saw him and he seemed to be walking just fine. I asked him how the ankle was and he told me that he hadn't really twisted it at all. He told me, "I did it to end the fight before someone got hurt." He added "Sergeant Thatcher (who was bigger than Gageiano) was swinging like he wanted to kill me."

When working the night shift the kitchen personnel would bring the midnight meal down to the motor pool in large thermos-type containers and we would form a chow line much like in the mess hall itself. They had the guys assigned to KP along as well to help. The KPs, or kitchen police (In the Army "policing" meant cleaning up) were rotated daily. It was looked upon as distasteful duty that luckily only came about once every few months. It was shared by the whole Company; everyone had his turn.

After a few days of seeing Gageiano behind the chow line and wearing "whites" I thought he was on some kind of punishment detail, since KP was often used as punishment for minor infractions. I asked him, "What's with the KP?"

He told me, "I asked the Captain to take me off driving a LARC because my nerves can't handle it."

That came as a shock to me because he didn't seem the type who would have much fear. But, unlike some of the would-be tough guy types, Gageiano was a standup guy and never was subjected to ridicule.

Everyone knew he had given it his best shot.

And yet another guy requested to be given different duty rather than operations in the South China Sea; he was transferred to the maintenance platoon and became a mechanic. He too was still respected because he hadn't acted like a badass.

I was surprised that the Army accommodated these two guys who were ultimately given an alternative assignment rather than treating them as, or charging them with cowardice, a serious charge in a Hostile Fire Zone, or "combat zone" as all of Vietnam was designated. I used to see posters saying "The Army Takes Care of Its Own." This now seemed to ring true.

I had been suffering a pain in the sole of my left foot starting back at Fort Story, Virginia. I didn't want to see an Army doctor, having heard stories about them and dentists as well. By the time we got to Vietnam and were working twelve hours a day, seven days a week the foot started hurting pretty bad and was swelling at times. So, one morning, coming off of the night shift I headed down to the Army dispensary in Cam Ranh Bay. I got to see an Army Captain, a doctor, and he looked at my foot. He said, "It looks like a plantar wart. There are no foot doctors at the Army dispensary but the Air Force has one." He wrote out a prescription for me to have my foot examined by the Air Force foot doctor.

I hitchhiked out to the Air Force Base, found the dispensary and went in. Two very nice Air Force Lieutenants looked at the foot and started to scrape away some of the callous with a scalpel. They kept asking if it hurt and I assured them that it didn't. Since it was raining that day I was wearing my rain gear. The rain gear was plain olive drab with no insignia. It was getting too warm to wear in the dispensary so I removed it. The Air Force officers now realized, looking at the insignias on my uniform, that they were treating a soldier rather that an airman. One of them joked, "Hey look at this guy, he's a trooper, just give him a bullet to bite on."

Hopefully he was joking.

They did more scraping and gave me a small bottle of some kind of acid to apply to dissolve away the plantar wart. They also gave me some instructions to give to the Army doctor should I need to return for further treatment. I used up the acid and a couple of days later returned to the Army dispensary. I got to see another doctor who looked at the note given me by the Air Force doctors. He read it, balled it up and threw it in the trash. He called in a medic and said, "Take this soldier inside and cut that thing out of his foot. He may need Novocain."

I lay down on a gurney with my bare foot against the medic's chest while he repeatedly injected my foot with Novocain. It hurt like hell! Once it was numb the medic took a scalpel and cut out the plantar wart. The front of his white tunic was very bloody, and a guy seated next to me with his hand immersed in a small tub of some sudsy stuff said, "I'll wait outside" and took his suds out into the hall.

The medic put a large bandage on the sole of my foot and declared me done. It felt like he made a half inch hole in the sole of my foot. I could hardly get my boot on over the bandage but finally managed it. I thought it might be a good idea to get a light duty note from the doctor since it was approaching evening and getting to be time to start my next night shift.

I was told the captain had left, and I would have to wait until his relief came in. I decided I had had enough and started limping my way back to my Company area, figuring my sergeant would assign me to light duty after telling him my surgery story.

The guys were already climbing aboard the LARC that would transport them down to the beach to perform the night shift. I saw my platoon sergeant and approached him. I said, "Sergeant, I just came from the dispensary after being there all day, no sleep in the last twenty-four hours and having surgery on my foot so…"

That's as far as I got when he said, "Before we talk about your foot Capainolo, you better go and shave."

I was so pissed I just walked away and climbed on board to go to work. I didn't shave either, shoot me.

I was hopping around but I could manage driving. The foot was throbbing. When I got to the operations area on the beach for the midnight meal Lieutenant Doran saw me hopping around and asked, "What's the problem Capainolo, why are you limping?" I told him about my surgery. He asked me, "Did you tell Sergeant Raynor?"

I said, "I did and he told me, go and shave before we talk about your foot."

Lieutenant Doran told me, "I'll get another driver; you just spend the rest of the shift sitting in the cab."

My assistant driver was a guy named Muller from Des Moines Iowa. I've had him as an assistant before and having had experience with him I thought I would be better off by myself. It didn't take long to suffer the truth of that.

I stayed low and out of sight in the cab, Muller drove. While returning to our operations area on land I could hear a jeep's horn blowing, as if we were being chased. We got to the operations area and Muller parked the LARC. Then it hit the fan. Muller had cut off a jeep carrying several officers and he was getting reamed. Lieutenant Doran came to where Miller was getting chewed out but could offer no help because he was out-ranked by the irritate officers and could only apologize for what one of his men did.

Some more of Muller's accomplishments: Since water would wash across the cargo deck of a LARC, there were water tight panels to keep it out of the bilges. A certain type of deck wrench was needed to open the panels. The deck wrenches were getting a bit rare but I still had mine. Another LARC came alongside while we were in the water asking to use my deck wrench to check out a noise below his deck. Muller picked up my deck wrench and tossed it to the other LARC. He threw short and my deck wrench went to the bottom of the bay.

We had side curtains that could be fitted to the LARC for carrying loose cargo that might otherwise slip off the deck. The side curtains were made of a heavy plastic that resembled a swimming pool liner with three lengths of steel cable running through it for strength. The curtains fit the length of the cargo area on each side and were made fast by a lever at one end that pulled the curtain tight and secure. One night we were going to carry loose cargo so I asked Miller to put on the side curtains. As he was attempting this not so difficult task, he dropped one of the curtains into the water and I watched it sink out of sight.

A request came along to transfer six soldiers from various companies to participate in the creation of a new unit that would carry cannons up and down a river, sort of a floating fire base. Sergeant Raynor used this opportunity to get rid of some people he didn't want in his platoon.

Goodbye to Muller.

With similar circumstances Sergeant Raynor was able to rid the second platoon of Bobby Ballor. He was a bass player from Massachusetts and a fun guy all around. He used to call beers "throats" and cigarettes "lungs." I have no idea why. Anyway, I never knew why Sergeant Raynor wanted to be rid of him but he did. Many, many years later I got a telephone call from Bobby. We talked for a while and he seemed very affected by the war. Some weeks later I got a phone call from his sister who told me Bobby had killed himself with an overdose of pills.

R.I.P. Bobby.

I met and befriended another soldier who came from Colorado in the snow and skiing country. He had a real deep radio announcer's kind of voice. His LARC number was 222 and he would mix it up at times saying, "Control this is 2, 2, 2, or 2 2- 2, or 2- 22." His name was Tom Edwards and he was called "T.E." He was an intelligent person but was low on self-esteem. He had a bad case of acne and this contributed to his being depressed at times. He and I were both fans of the book, *The Catcher in the Rye* by J.D. Salinger. We would often quote lines from the book. The main character in the book was Holden Caulfield and T.E. could have been him in real life. When I was leaving to go home T.E. wanted to take my place driving the jeep and being the mail clerk. I spoke with the First Sergeant and recommended him for the job. First Sergeant Whitefield took him as second platoon driver based upon my referral. After just two days of the new assignment T.E. told me that First Sergeant Whitefield had told him, "If you want to keep this job you're going to have to be looking sharp like Capainolo." I left the 165th that week hoping that he would work out. My mother had sent me a letter that arrived after my departure, so T.E. sent it back to me and wrote on the envelope, "Sawadee Cap", the Thai greeting.

I remember T.E. telling me that when he went home after BCT the first thing his mother said to him when meeting him at the airport was, "Oh Tom, your face." That hurt him deeply. I got a call from George Wilson, Ron Barrister and Bates, of all people, saying that they called for T.E. at his home in Colorado wanting to ask if he would like to join them in returning to Thailand now, as civilians, and open a big club for GIs. They were told that Tom had died of carbon monoxide poisoning, self-inflicted.

R.I.P. T.E. "222"

Chapter 15

We really did have great duty with the 165th. We drove on the water and on the land. It was hot but I'm sure it must have been much hotter inland. When it got really hot I would dip my hat into the water, filling it and place it on my head, letting the water spill down over me. Sometimes I would trade shifts with someone in order to stay on nights when it was much cooler, albeit a bit more challenging.

We used to buy cold sodas from a whacky guy who worked in a communications shack on the beach alongside our motor pool. The guy had a small refrigerator that he kept stocked with sodas and he sold them for profit. I stopped in a few times without incident. However, one day he wouldn't give me my change. It was a very small amount of money, but on principle I just couldn't let it just pass. I told him I wanted the change.

He picked up a carpenters' hatchet and came around a counter and advanced on me. I pushed my hands at his chest to fend him off, but he was a heavy guy and I was pinned against a wall. I finally got my right arm freed and socked him in his left temple. The blow backed him off just enough for me to wiggle free. Since he had a weapon and I didn't, I started for the door. Some instinct told me to hug the wall at the last second rather than go straight. The hatchet struck the door as I approached it. The son of a bitch had thrown it at my back. I got the hell out of there and didn't report it to anyone in authority, but I did tell my friend Charlie Lawton. He told me a few other guys had problems with him as well. They had gotten together and had, "taken care of it." The guy was replaced in the "Commo. Shack" and I never saw him again. I'm sure he wasn't gone as a result of having been "taken care of" since there was no inquiry. I did hear that he was relieved because he was nuts.

Who needed the Viet Cong to worry about when you had whacky Signal Corps. guys?

Coming from a very developed area like New York City and Long Island where there was a lot of illumination, I was amazed at how dark it was in Vietnam. Heading out to a ship was not too difficult since the ships sitting at anchor always had lights on in order not to be a hazard to navigation. The enemy did not have much in the way of boats so the ships were safe and had people on watch for approaching boats. The difficult part was finding your way back across the bay in the inky blackness of night. We finally started building a fire on our beach and it proved to be a good means of navigating our way home. It was also good for cooking steaks.

At times we carried foodstuffs rather than bombs and bullets. Steaks were in boxes approximately two square feet and six inches deep. The boxes had steel wire wrapped around them and were coated with some kind of wax. The rules were, if a box of any kind of foodstuffs were to fall into the water it could not be used to feed the troops and should be discarded. Somehow, some boxes would manage to fall into the water, with a little help of course, and we couldn't see why it should be wasted so we had some great BBQs. Steaks, ice cream and beer were the favorites.

I remember going out to a ship we were going to take on cargo from but had to wait for the hatches to be opened. That left us with nothing to do but bob around the ship. The captain of the ship called out to us and invited us to the galley for a breakfast of bacon, eggs and pancakes. Real eggs, not the powdered eggs we ate in our mess hall. There must have been a dozen of us floating around, and we backed our LARCs against the ship. Since the stern of a LARC is straight across and is about ten feet wide, if you backed it against the ship and let it idle in reverse it would stay stationary. We also butted them up against each other, side by side, and you could walk across the decks like it was a pontoon bridge. We climbed up the ship's gangway (or ladder for you landlubbers) and made our way to the galley. The ship's crew had already finished breakfast and the galley was cleaned up. "Breakfast is over" the cook said, so we started making our way back to the gangway to return to our LARCs.

We ran into the captain who asked "How did you have breakfast so fast?" We told him, "The cook turned us away since the galley was closed." The captain then went into the galley and told the cook to "start breakfast up again and feed these soldiers with whatever they wanted."

Thank you captain, I would never forget your kindness to a bunch of young soldiers.

Operations were conducted 24/7. We had 2, 12 hour shifts each day from 6:00 AM to 6:00 PM and from 6:00 PM to 6:00AM or in military time from 0:600 to 18:00 and from 18:00 to 0:600. We were safe from the enemy but not safe from accidents of which we had too many. I fell victim to an accident myself. I was wearing a ring against advice given to us. One night as I parked my LARC for the midnight meal I shut down the engine and jumped off steadying myself by placing my hand on the hoisting point. The hoisting point was simply a horseshoe-shaped ring where cables could be affixed in order to be able to lift the LARC with a crane. There were four of them, with two on either side, so the LARC would stay level and secure while being lifted. The hoisting point did not have sharp edges but was sharp enough to catch my ring as I jumped down the five or so feet to the ground. The ring buried itself into my ring finger and lifted a flap of skin to the first crease on the underside. If I had been shorter or the LARC higher, I might have pulled my finger off.

I pushed the flap of skin back down in its place and reported to Lieutenant Doran who had me taken by jeep to the Army dispensary. Upon arrival I explained the wound to a medic who brought me into a treatment room. A small Vietnamese guy wearing a doctor's lab coat started checking out the finger. I said, "Wait a minute," and went back out to where the Army medic was and asked, "Who is this guy?"

The medic assured me that, "he is a Vietnamese doctor and is fully capable."

I went back into the treatment room and the doctor had me soak my hand in some white sudsy stuff I took to be a kind of disinfectant. He then took my hand and placed some kind of cutting tool under my ring and advised me he was going to cut it off. The ring, not the finger. I said, "no" and he said, in his Vietnamese accent, "maybe infection." I told him, "Don't worry about it" and he dressed the wound with the ring still on. It did get infected so I got some iodine at the PX and kept dousing the wound with it, and the finger healed up very well. The doctor was good or the Army wouldn't have him treating American troops. I was sorry I doubted that, just based on his not being American.

One morning the call came to the 165th that there was a group of Vietnamese who worked for the Army as maids and general service people that needed to be picked up across the bay and brought over to our side. They were usually picked up and transported every morning by LCM landing craft but for some reason the LCMs were not available. The call went out for volunteers to cross the bay in our LARCs and bring the people in. I say volunteers because we were told that the village contained known Viet Cong. That's all we needed to hear and everyone wanted to go. I was one of the lucky ones picked and we got the order to "mount up," to make the trip with Sergeant Taffe taking the lead.

We donned our helmets and flak jackets, not normally worn, and headed out across a very dark bay, full throttle, in a loose, six abreast formation. It was exciting and a break from our normal duty.

When we got to the dock a crowd of about eighty-five Vietnamese were waiting. It was chaos; people started indiscriminately jumping onto the LARCs that listed so much we were in danger of capsizing. We got the mob of people under control by chasing them off the LARCs then making them come aboard in an orderly fashion, each LARC taking twenty to thirty-five people. Soon, we crossed back and delivered the people without mishap. We did not draw any hostile fire.

Another interesting duty that took some of us away from our daily activities was to carry fresh water out to a small island that had no natural supply. The island was protecting the entrance to the bay and was manned by Republic of Korea Marines. We called them ROK Marines. Water was loaded onto my LARC in fifty-five gallon drums. I crossed the bay and drove up onto the beach. ROK Marines were there to mount my vehicle and guide me to where the water drop offs were located. Following their directions, I stopped at each water depository, and the ROK Marines would dump the water from the deck of the LARC into their containers.

The ROK Marines were allies but still could be scary. Their language and actions were gruff and sounded excited compared to Americans. One time I left the beach at our operations area and headed out to their island encampment with two enlisted ROK Marines and one officer aboard. The two enlisted men made themselves comfortable on the deck over the bow and forward of the windshield. Riding in this area was forbidden due to safety regulations. I soon got a radio call from our control dispatch that usually monitored operations with binoculars telling me to, "Get those men off the bow." I slowed down and gestured to the two Marines to come back to the cargo deck. They refused, I kept asking them, in pantomime, since they spoke no English and I spoke no Korean, to move. They seemed somewhat belligerent. I looked at the officer, who, so far, had nothing to say. I turned the LARC back to a heading for the beach. This prompted the officer to order his men back to the cargo deck as directed. I turned back to a heading for the island.

Once we got to the island we went to where the ROK Marines were camped. They lived in a hole in the ground that looked to be about ten feet square, deep enough for them to walk around in and with a roof of corrugated metal. I saw them gesturing to me to come down into their bunk area; there was something they wanted to show me. It made me nervous after the foredeck incident, and the officer was gone. It turned out they wanted me to see the skin of a leopard or some other big spotted cat they apparently had killed and skinned. After I admired the cat's pelt we all started to get along better. The gruffness was really just part of their mannerisms and speech; they were actually a friendly bunch.

They showed me a homemade barbell they had made by using a tree branch thick enough to be the bar and the ends were wrapped with barbed wire to act as the weights. I picked it up a bit and found that it weighed maybe a hundred pounds. From doing some limited weight lifting back home I knew I could clean and jerk the barbell with one arm. I did it and they were quite impressed. Of course, I was much bigger than any of them and probably outweighed them by about forty pounds. The next test I was subjected to was to punch a canvas wrapped piece of wood that had been nailed to a tree. I hit it pretty good, again relying on my greater size.

After that we were all buddies.

One night I got together with my good friend Joe Callahan and we hitch-hiked down to the Enlisted Men's Club or EM club. Hitchhiking was easy; there was a lot of vehicle traffic since Cam Ranh Bay was a major transportation and logistics center. Army vehicles would ordinarily stop and give you a lift. The drinks were ten cents each and I had several rum and Cokes. Never being much of a drinker I got drunk pretty quickly. Rum has a curious effect on me. I get sort of numb and my lips feel like they are made of rubber. You could probably take out my appendix after a couple of shots.

Anyway, Joe and I started walking back to our Company area and were quickly picked up by a GI driving a three quarter ton truck. I remember running up to the stopped truck and diving right over the tailgate, landing on a bunch of gasoline cans known as Gerri cans. Like I said, no pain. When the truck driver reached his destination we got out and continued our hitch-hiking. We saw a LARC coming down the road and waved him down. It was from the 165th and I knew the driver whose name was Sandhoff. Climbing aboard, our journey continued. We came across two soldiers hitch-hiking and Sandhoff stopped to pick them up. They were amazed with the LARC never having seen one before. Sandhoff asked them, "Where is your unit located?" They pointed to the top of a mountain. We had seen the mountain during our stay at Cam Ranh Bay and had seen the red lights shining at its summit. They told us, "Its a radar installation and there is a road wide enough for the LARC to be driven up to the top." Driving up would save them the steep climb and show the "boat on wheels" to their buddies. Even though I was drunk I didn't think it was a good idea. The other guys did however, and away we went.

The road up to the installation was just wide enough for the LARC. The side of the road overlooking the ever increasing drop-off looked very crumbly and loose. Suddenly I was sober. I stayed on the opposite side of the drop-off thinking I could jump if the need arose. By some miracle, or incredibly good luck, we made it to the top. People came running out of their tents to see the LARC. Now, to turn around was another challenge. We had to go back and forth, making a three point turn into a nine or ten point turn. Coming down the mountain road was worse than going up. Fifteen tons of LARC wanted to take off down the steep incline and Sandhoff was standing on the brake pedal. We could smell brakes burning. I told Sandhoff to use the third pedal located next to, and left of the brake. This pedal was designed to hold back a LARC to some degree when descending a steep incline, carrying a heavy load. It didn't use brakes to accomplish this. We called it a drag pedal.

We saved the brakes and made it down safely. We found out later that Sandhoff had tunnel vision. I think I had it too that night, keeping my eyes riveted on the sandy steep and unstable road ahead and not daring to look to the side.

Chapter 16

Day to day operations were straightforward and could get boring, so some levity or pranks were bound to take place. The LARC had drain holes in the bottom of the bilge about the size of a fifty-cent piece. They could be unscrewed, allowing for drainage of the bilge. The bilge pumps pumped water out at an amazing speed and velocity. The water would be pumped overboard at points left and right and to the rear of the LARC. The ports were about three inches in diameter, like a fire hose. The idea was to go out into the water with the drain holes opened so the LARC would take on water to be used as "ammunition." If you aimed the bilge pump ports at a specific target and flipped on the bilge pump toggle switches located on the dash board the target would get doused by a heavy and powerful stream of water. One of the most memorable targets to get doused in this manner was our own Sergeant Raynor while sitting in a jeep. I had a clue this might happen when I saw one of our guys giving signals to a LARC driver to move to get aligned with the "target." It was a perfect shot and Sergeant Raynor got drenched. He took it all in fun and probably got cooled off a bit.

The latrine at the company area had six seats but the ones in operations areas like the motor pool had smaller two seat versions. Since we were operating on the beach we had sand all around. In the Army the latrines were assigned for officer, NCO, and finally enlisted men. Sergeant Chessman was at the motor pool on the beach one day and headed for the NCO latrine. No one had noticed that the wind had shifted sand and created a void under the rear of the latrine. It must have been teetering as result and as Sergeant Chessman sat, it toppled over. You can imagine the unimaginable.

A LARC came ashore one day with a remora fish stuck to its bow. It was about eighteen inches long and stuck to the LARC by the suction disk on top of its head. I thought it was gruesome. Some guys, braver than most, tried to pull it off. It wouldn't come loose and had to be pried off with a knife. These fish typically attach to sharks so what does that tell you about the waters we were operating in?

Racing was always fun too, either on land or in the water. One night having completed our last mission and finding the ship closing up its hatches, Charlie Lawton and I headed back to the beach. It was night and we, each driving our own LARCs with no passengers, were soon racing. Since it was dark you had to be especially alert not to run into another vessel. The LCMs were a particular danger because if one was coming directly at you, the ramp on the front blocked your vision of its running lights. There was always a variety of vessels in the area and we saw an LST anchored some distance from us. An LST is a large landing craft capable of carrying tanks. It had a small crew that stayed on the craft around the clock and had sleeping quarters. The LST was sitting at anchor. They must have had a surprise awakening when Charlie's LARC slammed into their anchor chain with a big clang. Charlie's LARC was stopped dead in the water but we very quickly left as people came out on deck and started hollering at us. The LARC only suffered a bent handrail on the forward deck.

On one particularly calm night out in the South China Sea, we arrived at the ship we were to take cargo from but the hatches had not been opened yet. This usually took an hour or more before we began taking on cargo. There were about ten LARCs bobbing around, with guys just waiting and carrying on conversations. One of the LARC's was being driven by Roy Bates who became known as "Master Bates." He was a special case, no doubt suffering some mental illness, and should not have been in the Army. Anyway, he was alone that night; he fell asleep and began to drift off. No one paid any attention since he was always doing some crazy stunt or another. I started to get concerned when we could no longer see him and voiced my concern to the other guys. They basically said, "Sorry 'bout that." Since there was no enemy around getting lost was the biggest problem Bates would have to face. Everybody had radio contact with the rest of the Company and Dispatch, known on the radio as "Control." If he was in trouble he could easily call for assistance. The thinking was that if a helicopter needed to be called in to find him he would get into some kind of jam and possibly it would come to the Army's attention that he was off the rails.

Well, that didn't happen and he had found his own way back and made it to midnight chow with no one in authority being the wiser. He told us, "I was sleeping, and all of a sudden the LARC started bumping around. That woke me up and I could make out in the dark that I was on the rocks at the base of a mountain, I was gunning the LARC forward and reverse, *vroom*, *vroom*. When the tide rose I finally broke free. I had a hard time finding my way back but didn't want to get on the radio so I was lost for hours."

A call went out to transfer some troops for TDY (Temporary Duty Assignment) some coming from each unit in the battalion to go to Nha Trang. Naturally, Sergeant Raynor picked Bates as an opportunity to be rid of him. Nha Trang was a place that could be dangerous. After several weeks Bates came back to the 165th with stories of getting mortared and rocketed. He had a flak jacket he was issued temporarily in his locker that he neglected to turn in upon leaving Nha Trang.

As crazy as Bates could be he did save a guy from drowning and should have been given the Soldiers Medal for an act of heroism not connected to combat. I had been at a presentation of the Soldiers Medal for a soldier who had pulled his buddy out of a burning vessel.

Bates' act of heroism happened at a Special Services beach we were permitted to go to while off duty. Sometimes a LARC would be assigned to lifeguard duties at the beach, but not always, and not on this day.

One of our guys had swum out pretty far and was having trouble making it back to the beach. He started to yell for help and it was obvious he was going down. Bates had brought along his inflatable rubber mattress known as a "rubber lady." He started for the surf and quickly ran back to get the mattress. He dived into the surf with it; he lay down on his stomach and paddled out like you would on a surfboard. He reached the drowning soldier and they both made it back to shore, using the mattress as a raft to hang on to.

Had the rescue been related to our platoon sergeant or Lieutenant Doran, I believe he would have been a candidate for the medal. No one denied him the medal; it was just a matter of no one thinking of it at the time.

The effectiveness of the operations of the 165[th.] was measured by how much cargo we moved on each shift. Careful records were kept on how many trips were made between a ship and the cargo's destination, most often to the Air Force's ammunition dump. There were three LARC companies operating in Cam Ranh Bay. By this time, we had some experience under our belts and were no longer intimidated by the other company's moves to get alongside the ship and get the stevedore to jump on their LARC rather than ours. There were no rules; the stevedore would jump on to the closest LARC.

One fine day, as we prepared to start our shift the word got around to not let any other company get in for a load. This was done by running interference for each other and cutting off rivals from getting in close enough to pick up a stevedore who didn't have any stake in the competition but who would just transfer onto the closest LARC that could be bordered safely. We learned that even if another LARC managed to get alongside the ship under the boom we could make contact with the stern of that LARC and simply push it out of the spot. This went on for the entire shift and as a result we moved hundreds of tons, and we were told the other company moved zero! At the end of the shift our captain called for a Company formation and told us, "I got a call from the other LARC company's commanding officer telling me what had gone on." He then said, "The fun is over, and you are ordered not to repeat this action." As he gave us the command to, "fall out," I think I noticed a faint smile on the faces of the officers.

Soon after we found ourselves in kind of a reverse action. The speed limit for vehicles was thirty-miles per hour. The LARC had a maximum speed on land of thirty-five miles per hour. We usually drove with the accelerator pressed to the floor which did not over-tax the engine because it had a governor on it that kept the RPM's at a safe level. The problem started when MPs began handing out speeding violations for exceeding thirty miles per hour.

The reason we "speed demons" exceeded the limit was because we typically drove standing up. There were three separate seats in the LARC's cab but we drove with our heads out of the tops of the cab with our right arms resting on top of the windshield. We steered with our left hand and operated the foot pedals with our left foot. If we tried to drive with our accelerator only depressed enough to make thirty miles per hour the bouncing of the LARC would cause us to be erratic on the pedal, with the LARC surging and slowing. The LARC had no suspension but just rode on huge soft tires and the bouncing could get extreme.

So what we did was stage a slowdown and traveled at low speed whenever on land. The sergeants and officers soon realized what was happening and rode up and down the now convoy of slowly moving LARCs, urging us to pick up the speed. We were taught that while operating a LARC we were in command of that vehicle and, as such, had the final word on its operation. This included having authority over even a general, (yeah, try that sometime) but I think that only applied when in the water. Anyhow, we cited the dangers of carrying bombs if we were not allowed to operate the vehicle as we best knew how. The slow up affected the tonnage reports so the MPs were called off and we went back to our flat out thirty-five miles per hour.

Strange how we had gotten away with our protest but, after all, it was the 1960's.

One night Charlie Lawton and I were assigned to guard a huge barge loaded ten feet high with bombs and mortar rounds. Our instructions were that if any boat approached the barge we were to fire warning shots over their heads and yell *"did maio,"* which translated in English is "go away quickly." If a boat kept coming, we were to fire on it and its occupants. Crazy as it may sound, and probably crazy as it was, we both smoked cigarettes while dangling our legs and arms over the side of the barge, thinking if a hot ash or butt fell it would land in the water. We took turns sleeping wherever we could get comfortable, laying on bombs and crates of mortars. While Charlie was sleeping I saw a boat approaching and could tell that it was a tugboat. Knowing the enemy didn't have tugboats that I had ever seen or heard of, I didn't fire or challenge them to stop. The tugboat was marked with the logo of Alaska Barge and Transport, which was a civilian contractor hired by the U.S. to augment operations in Cam Ranh Bay and in other places up and down the coast of Vietnam.

The tug was tied up alongside the barge and I could see a cigarette glowing up in the wheelhouse. I heard someone call to me, "Come on up and get a cup of coffee." I boarded the boat cautiously and found the ladder well to get up to the tiny galley. The boat's captain got me coffee and asked me "Where are you from? "How long have you been in Vietnam?" Just making conversation. He asked me, "What kind of rifle are you carrying? Can I have a look at it?" I told him, "It's an M 14." I had not chambered a round and I pulled the magazine out before handing him the weapon. American or not, I was a good enough soldier to know better than to hand a stranger a loaded rifle. I thanked him for the coffee and asked, "Can my buddy come up for some coffee?"

He said, "Sure." I made my way back down to the tug's deck and then back onto the barge. Charlie went up and spoke with the tug boat captain much the same as I had.

In a similar situation I was assigned guard duty in our motor pool and operations area during the Vietnamese Tet holiday of 1967. Extra security was in place because the enemy was known to launch offenses during this holiday period. Our operations area went right down to the shoreline where LARCs entered and exited the water. There was a pier that ran out for about thirty yards into the water. While I was manning my post a small Vietnamese boat approached the pier and made itself fast to it. I was resting my rifle against the wheel of a LARC and had it trained on the boat. Sergeant Raynor came along, "Hey, Cap, do you see that boat?" He wanting to know if I had the Vietnamese boat covered. I said, "Sarge, you're giving away our position, calling out for me."

There was an MP post at the entrance to the motor pool, I was relieved when the MPs drove down the pier in a jeep and checked out the Vietnamese.

I learned, or maybe confirmed, something that night, having had my rifle trained on people, safety off and ready to fire. I felt that if they made any aggressive move that would potentially hurt any of my buddies I certainly would have gunned them down. They were very exposed if they tried to come in over the flat sand beach or climb and run down the length of the pier. And then there were the MPs close by who would have joined me in defending the motor pool. The best thing happened, or didn't happen. The Vietnamese were not hostile and I didn't have to shoot anyone.

Of the three LARC companies operating at Cam Ranh Bay ours, the 165th, was the best. Our vehicles were better maintained and performed and looked as much. Most of the credit for being the best belonged to a thirty-three-year veteran who was in charge of all maintenance on our vehicles. He was a warrant officer we called "Tuffy" and with good reason. He was a no-nonsense officer who would lock your heels (make you stand at attention) and chew you out for even the smallest failure of your job performance. On one occasion he was chewing out a soldier and had locked his heels. The soldier had a slight grin on his face knowing we were watching. Tuffy started to turn away but stopped and looked back at the soldier and said, "You better wipe that smile off your face or you'll be smiling from behind bars."

Get the picture?

We were told that a General Blander was coming from his command in Thailand to inspect the three LARC companies. He was going to have his pick as to which one would be transferred to his command. Of course, with what he could see and our stellar record for moving war material, he picked us to go.

We were not happy about this prospect. Most of us were not happy with the cut in pay we would receive by moving to an area not designated as a Hostile Fire Zone. My pay as a Specialist E-4 would get reduced from approximately $240.00 per month to approximately $160.00. Some guys felt that we would not be contributing as much to the war effort. And there was George Wilson who kept saying, "There's no glory in Thailand." A lot of guys were filling out form 1049s which is a request for transfer, saying they wanted a transfer to the 1st Cavalry Air Mobile Division. The rumor was that they needed door gunners on their helicopters because the gunners had a combat life expectancy of three seconds.

That was probably a little more glory than even George could handle.

George was an interesting guy. He spoke with a heavy British accent because his parents moved the family to England when George, who was born in the U.S., was an infant. They returned to the U.S. when he was eighteen and being a U.S citizen, he was drafted. He was a real party guy and told us a lot of stories about England where there were "Teddy Boys and Rockers." This was at the peak of the British rock and roll invasion.

Anyway, Captain Posner called for a formation of the entire Company and explained that, "There is a real need for our type of operations in Thailand. We all have a critical MOS (military occupational specialty) and, as such, no transfers would be granted to the 1st Cavalry or anywhere else."

We broke down our camp and loaded everything to be shipped to Camp Vayama in Sattahip, Thailand by sea and the troops by C-130 aircraft.

The airplane ride was an experience. We were trucked out to the Air Force Base at Cam Ranh Bay where the first group of our people bordered the plane. More planes and troops would follow to get the entire company moved in. The seats in the plane were just netting, like on patio furniture, but looser. It looked like a scene in the movies where you see paratroopers ready to jump. We took off and climbed quickly. The ramp at the rear of the plane was left wide open and we could look out and see Vietnam from our bird's eye view. As we approached our first stop, which was Saigon, we descended very quickly. My ears started to hurt alarmingly. I looked around and saw several guys keeling over in their seats and cupping their hands over their ears. I looked at the pilots, who I could see through the open cockpit door, and they looked fine. Thankfully, the pain went away once we were lower and landed.

As was explained to us by the plane's pilot when questioned about the earache, "It happened because when flying over Vietnam we stayed as high as possible to avoid ground fire." When pilots approached their destination they dived, descending rapidly, to limit the time spent in ground fire range. The next stop was Utapao Royal Thai Air Force Base.

Once on the ground we bordered a bus that would take us to our Company area at Camp Vayama. An officer got on the bus and welcomed us to Thailand. He gave us a little talk on what the mission was at the Air Force Base and said that, "We all wear a purple uniform here." The guys looked around, what the hell was a he talking about, purple uniforms? He was just saying that there was intra-service cooperation with Army, U.S. Air Force, and Thai Royal Air Force all working together.

Some guys just didn't get it.

Once we got to our new Company area at Camp Vayama we were surprised how nice it was compared to our billets in Vietnam. The barracks were nice and airy with screens and jalousie like slats letting in air. The barracks were constructed of wood that looked like redwood stained patio furniture. The Enlisted Men's Club was nearby.

As we had formation in the company street guys who had been there for their entire overseas tour yelled out the windows, "New blood." This, because upon getting ready to move from Vietnam to Thailand, we all had been given new uniforms to replace what we had worn out in Vietnam. The new uniforms did not yet have any insignia of rank or who we were.

The "Old-timers" were soon to find out.

A number of our guys went to the Enlisted Man's or "EM" club and were enjoying some long awaited beers. Between the drinking and going back at some soldiers who didn't yet know who we were, a few scuffles started. Somehow, Bates was right in the middle of it. The EM's manager must have made a call because a number of MP's came to the club and started ordering us back to our barracks. Bates was still instigating and the MPs followed him into our barracks. He got into a push and shove with one of them and had him in a headlock. I can remember the MP's helmet liner falling off of his head and rolling down the aisle. The MP retrieved his helmet liner and began making his way out. Joe Callahan asked one of the MPs, "How many guys are in your MP Company?" He said, "A hundred and twenty-five"

Joe told him, "You're 'gonna need more than that."

The next morning, we were made to fall out into ranks. The MP that had trouble with Bates walked up and down each squad with his sergeant in an effort to identify who had grappled with him. He stopped in front of Bates and looked directly at him for several seconds, then moved on. He made no identification although I'm sure he knew it was Bates. I never could figure out why he didn't ID Bates and I thought, there went another chance to be rid of him.

I had developed a cough and since we were still waiting for our vehicles it was no problem getting on sick call. I met Lieutenant Doran at the dispensary. He had an ear infection complicated from the airplane ride. The doctor told him he had a cold that got driven into his inner ear due to the pressure on the plane.

I got checked out by a medic who gave me some cough medicine and told me to come back in a couple of days. Since I was still coughing a couple of days later I again went on sick call. This time I was given a TB test and told to come back yet again to have the TB test evaluated, then the medics sent me in to see the doctor.

He looked at my history and said, "This is the third time you've been here, you must be doing a lot of coughing." He said it with a tone that was accusatory, as if I was a malingerer.

I explained to him that, "I only came on my own on the first visit. Each subsequent visit was as ordered by the medics." I got no response, not a nod, an O.K. or anything. He gave me some pills and away I went. Air Force doctors were nicer.

Thank you, Captain Queeg (Humphrey Bogart, *"The Caine Mutiny").*

Soon after, our LARCs began arriving, having been transported from Cam Ranh Bay, Vietnam, to Sattahip, Thailand. A number of LARCs had been driven off the shore onto an LST's ramp back at Cam Ranh Bay into the cavernous interior of the vessel. The LST sailed around with the ramp wide open. Obviously the hinge point of the LST's ramp was above water level. Upon arriving off the shore of Sattahip we lined up in the center of the cargo area and were told to gun the LARC right off the LST and splash down. If you went too slow the LARC's stern would hit the leading edge of the ramp, causing damage. I was one of the soldiers driving a LARC off the LST. I thought at first it was crazy but it turned out to be a great adventure with the giant splash it made.

Other LARCs came, having been loaded onto ships. They were being off-loaded from a ship tied to a dock, and at night. It was amazing to see these fifteen-ton vehicles being picked up off the ship and lowered to the dock by a crane. Cables were attached to the four hitching points and the LARC stayed almost level as it was being lowered. I was one of the guys assigned to drive these LARCs to a designated, temporary gravel covered area, where we parked them side by side.

We began operations at yet another temporary area where we had access to the water, this time the Gulf of Siam. The problem that arose at once was that the water was full of rocks. At first we had people sit on the bow of a LARC and act as guides as we threaded our way through the rocks.

We had one soldier who had been a diver at his home in Florida, and he was a great help by marking a channel through the rocks using empty painted oil cans. He dove down and tied the floating cans to the rocks. We asked him, "Are you worried about sharks?"

He said, "I'm used to seeing them while diving in Florida." He said, "They don't usually attack if you don't bother with them or act like a wounded fish."

Anyhow, he never did get paid any attention to by the sharks. Even with having a safe channel laid out for us, and getting the guides back to driving their own LARCs, it was slow going and less cargo was getting moved. Each day we would pile twenty to thirty guys on a LARC at our parking area at Camp Vayama and get a ride to the area where the rocky beach was located. Once there we cranked up our LARCs and began operations.

While at camp Vayama I started having trouble with Bates. He had something going on in his head about his being from Chicago and me being from New York and who was the tougher as a result.

When I became the jeep driver for the second platoon leader I spent a lot of time in the Orderly Room (the Company office) where I would usually help the two clerks with typing up reports. On a list of troops serving in the 165th I noticed that Bates was in fact from Delaware and not Chicago. I never said anything about it, thinking if the delusional "Master Bates" wanted to hail from Chicago, who cares?

Bates' bunk was directly across the middle aisle from mine. I knew that he shaved with a straight razor. One night when he was drunk and being particularly weird he attacked me. I had been sleeping lightly with him being so close and I could hear his bare feet padding across the floor coming my way. I was afraid he might have that razor, at the ready, to cut my throat. He didn't. Instead, he grabbed at my throat in an attempt to choke me. I was able to get up and throw some punches at him, landing a few on his face. Manic as he was, it didn't have much effect. Some guys grabbed him and broke up the fight. One guy who had befriended Bates was able to talk him back to his bunk. I didn't get much sleep that night but had no further trouble. In the morning Bates had some pretty good bruises on his face but didn't remember a thing about it. He was heard yelling in the latrine as he looked at his face in the mirror, "What the hell happened to my face?"

The morning following the attack in the barracks Bates was driving the LARC taking us down to the operations area. As we were heading down to the beach the night shift was coming back. Bates started playing chicken with the oncoming LARCs by just easing over to the oncoming traffic. Sergeant Taffe was in charge and he kept telling Bates, "Move back over." He did but soon started playing his game again. I got over to the side away from the oncoming LARCs, thinking I could jump if there was a collision. We probably would all have been killed or seriously injured.

At about this time, the second platoon's jeep driver rotated back "stateside" or "back to the world" as we usually said. At a morning formation Sergeant Raynor asked who would like to be the jeep driver for Lieutenant Stone, our second platoon leader. Several people raised their hands, including me. I wasn't selected and Sandhoff, (who you might remember from our trip up the mountain back at Cam Ranh Bay), got the job. A few days later walking back to my tent Sergeant Raynor stopped me and asked, "Do you still want to drive the second platoon jeep?" I said, "Yes, and asked, "What happened to Sandhoff?" He told me that Sandhoff was driving Lieutenant Stone and they almost got creamed by a tank truck approaching from the side. The Lieutenant saw the tank truck and yelled at Sandhoff to stop. They didn't get hit but the Lieutenant thought Sandhoff should have easily seen the truck approaching. He thought maybe Sandhoff had a vision problem and sent him to be tested. It turned out that he had tunnel vision.

The Lieutenant was from Massapequa Park on Long Island and I was from Patchogue, Long Island. We both agreed that since I had experience driving on the Long Island Expressway, jeep driving in Thailand would be a piece of cake. In Thailand, however, they drove on the left side of the road, like in England. You might think driving on the opposite side of the road, from what we were used to, would take some adjusting. It didn't, you just pulled over to the left side and away you went. I even had to navigate a traffic circle in downtown Sattahip and had no problem.

For my R&R (rest and recuperation) I took the bus up to Bangkok with two guys from the 165[th.] It was a fairly long bus ride but we did stop at a bus terminal where we could get some refreshments and use the bathroom. When I walked into the lavatory

I was shocked to find women using the toilets. I went right back out but could not find any doors marked men or women. A couple of GIs walked past me and into the bathroom. I waited to see them come right out as I had but they stayed in there. Once again I entered the lavatory, soon understanding that men and women used the same facility. I thought it was because we were in rural areas, and a common bathroom was a good way to save some money. Later, I was at a large nightclub in downtown Bangkok and found the same thing.

While in Bangkok we followed some tips other guys who had been there gave us. They told us we could hire a cab for our entire three day stay for just six bottles of liquor. The driver would be available around the clock and act as a guide and interpreter as well. We also learned that the Capital Hotel was leased out in its entirety by the U.S. and, as such, was the same as being in barracks. The tip we got was, if the hotel was totally full we could go to another hotel and the US Army would be paying the bill. All we had to do was go to the Capital Hotel desk and express an interest in staying somewhere else and we were given a voucher. We then went to the Fortuna Hotel and checked in there.

The hotel was clean and had all the facilities we had been doing without, like hot water, showers and bathtubs, room service, flush toilets and a swimming pool. One thing it did have and I would not have missed was lizards. Even though we were many floors up the lizards were there, making the kissing sound that they did. We were used to seeing the lizards in our operations areas and knew they were harmless. We would pick them up and toss them to someone and they would grasp onto his uniform. If the guy was squeamish, he would freak out. It was a silly, fun thing we did.

We spent the three days in Bangkok, eating in fine restaurants and doing a lot of sightseeing. We saw many temples (or WATS in the Thai language), and they were magnificent. I still have all the 35 mm slides I took. One of the sights I saw was the Temple of the Golden Buddha. It is five and half tons of solid gold. An interesting story about this statue is that it had been covered over with plaster and stucco to hide the gold and prevent it from being stolen by invading armies throughout history. In 1954, while the statue was being moved, it accidentally fell and some of the plaster and stucco surface fell away. It was then discovered that the statue was solid gold and is the largest solid gold statue in the world. If you can stand the heat and humidity I would recommend visiting Bangkok.

Another interesting place we visited was a snake farm. There I saw many varieties of cobras as well as pythons. The king cobra we saw was ten feet long. Visitors were allowed to hold a large python across their shoulders and have pictures taken. I passed on that; snakes are not my favorite animals. We did learn that some kinds of snake venom were collected and was used for medical purposes. I still don't like them.

We would have visitors come out to our operations area to see the LARCs at times and take pictures of them. One jeep full of guys from Alaska Barge and Transport came out and when they entered the Orderly Room we were asked, "How do you guys live out here? We just ran over a Banded Krait just down the road." A Banded Krait is a particularly venomous, dangerous snake. I did a little research and found that Thailand has two hundred plus varieties of snake, sixty of them being venomous. We just shrugged it off saying, "We don't bother them and they don't bother us."

Staying on the snake topic, I had run over at least six snakes during my time driving a jeep. Being focused on the road while driving I would see the snakes crossing but if I had passengers they wouldn't see them unless I hollered "snake!" The First Sergeant had been with me when I ran over my first snake. It felt like driving over a garden hose. Sergeant Whitefield told me it didn't kill the snake unless I hit the brakes and skidded over it. So I was always ready to yell "snake!" everyone could brace up for the sudden application of the brakes. While driving Lieutenant Stone we came upon a Cobra and a Mongoose fighting right at the side of the road. It was quite a show but Lieutenant Stone wanted to get away from it, fearing that the snake might get into the jeep. If it had, I would be out. "Every man for himself."

At the hotel one evening I sat by the pool drinking a beer. A Thai woman stopped by and asked, "How do you like the hotel?" I recognized her as being a hostess and I invited her to join me. She sat down at my table. She asked, "What's your name and where are you from in America?"

I told her, "My name is Pat and I'm from New York." When you say New York there is usually a lot of interest. I asked her name and she said, it was "Moo" I said, "I'm not familiar with that name." she explained, "It's a nickname my brothers gave me, it means baby pig, and I was squealing like one when I had been bitten by a cobra in our home."

Thinking I would learn some native medical treatment I asked, "What do you do if bitten by a cobra?"

She looked at me like I was some kind of dope and said, "You go to the hospital."

Sounded like a good safety tip, I tried to remember it.

Chapter 17

By now we had our own working and living quarters some fourteen miles from Headquarters at Camp Vayama. The engineers had plowed a nice ramp-like excavation for LARCs entering and exiting the water. There was a tower built just high enough to step off right onto a LARC's deck making it easy to open the engine hatch and check fluid levels. One chore that needed to be done each time we exited the water was to grease the propeller hub because the lubricant became contaminated by salt water. The power steering units had to be greased as well and, to do this, the front wheels had to be turned fully one way and then the other so that the mechanic could access the grease points by kneeling in the wheel well. When the wheels needed to be turned the mechanic would knock on the aluminum hull with the grease gun as a signal to the driver to turn the wheels. This was the cause of an accident with a soldier being pinned in the wheel well by a five-foot wheel. It was thought that he, the mechanic had accidentally tapped the grease gun nozzle against the hull and the driver thought this was the signal to turn the wheel. His injuries were such that he left our Company and never returned. We did hear that he would recover.

The tower was also a work station for our dispatcher named Cleever. Of course we called him Beaver after the kid on the TV show; "Leave It to Beaver." The family name on the show was Cleaver as opposed to Cleever, but it was close enough.

Our living quarters were greatly improved by our resident carpenter "Smitty" building a wood frame for each tent rather than using tent poles and rope. They were like framed houses covered by canvas rather than shingles. When the tents were being finished, Smitty assigned the personnel who would occupy each tent. I was picked to be in the same tent as Bates. I made it known to a couple of other tent mates that, "With Bates being assigned to our tent, never sleeping and doing crazy things, none of us will get any rest." I went to Smitty and told him, "There is no way I was going to be in the same tent with Bates." Smitty gave me some argument but I was adamant so he finally assigned me to another tent. I was assigned to the last tent in line in the second platoon's row. Since all the other guys in my tent were LARC drivers with rotating day and night shifts, they would occupy the tent at night while on day shift and they were all out when on night shift, leaving me alone. As a jeep driver my shift was always days, it was O.K. with me. I learned that someone told Bates I refused be in the same tent with him and that probably further fueled his dislike for me. Sorry 'bout that.

Our operations were going well with many tons of material being loaded at ship-side and transported by sea and then overland to the intended destinations, but it was not without mishaps.

A forklift was loaded on to a LARC to be transported to a ship. The seas were rough that day and while alongside the ship, awaiting the cable to be lowered to attach to the forklift, it slid off the deck and sank to the bottom of Cam Ranh Bay. There were several bombs lost the same way. Drivers would at times call in to Dispatch and report that seas were too rough to continue operations but were often not heeded. I remember one day when there was no choice. I was at ship-side and had to move away because there were swells that must have been twenty feet high. It was a huge rolling sea and the LARC would ride up one side and slide down the other. When at the crest of the swells I could see the weather deck of the ship that was normally twenty-five or thirty feet above the waterline. It was quite a sight but not too scary because the swells did not break at all, thank God. We were ordered to return to base and made our way back to shore with a great story to tell.

A Merchant Marine sailor went missing off his ship and was thought to have fallen overboard. We were asked to search the area. We looked for a while and just when we were going to give up his body rose to the surface. He was pulled up onto the deck of a LARC and transported to the beach where an ambulance was waiting. The dead man had a wound on his head. It was thought that he might have hit his head somehow and went overboard, or someone whacked him on the head and threw him overboard. We never heard any final resolution.

We were not permitted to take merchant marine sailors, who were civilians, and ferry them to shore on our LARCs. They often asked for rides to and from the beach and, for the most part, we would take them. They wanted a break from their ships and a chance to go downtown to the bars on the strip. We warned them not to be alone while on the strip because it was not uncommon for lone people to be jumped, beaten and robbed. GIs knew this and stayed together when downtown. I remember one sailor who was begging for a ride out to his ship because he had been attacked with a machete. I had never seen such long cuts or as many stitches on anyone, not then and not to this date. He was definitely given a ride out to his ship.

Bates, of course, was up to his weird antics. One night a few friends and I arrived back at our tents after being downtown. We came upon Bates walking around wearing a sheet as a robe and a crown made out of some vines with leaves. He looked like Nero and acted just as demented. We said, "How you doing, Bates," and his response was, "Hunka." Whatever was said to him got the same response, "Hunka." How could you sleep in peace with that going on? On another occasion, in the middle of the night, he took a tank truck, and went speeding around the Company area and headed to downtown Sattahip to score some marijuana. He wasn't even in uniform and somehow evaded the MPs. Again, an opportunity missed to say goodbye to him.

While returning from being off-loaded on land, one of our LARCs went off the road when trying to make a ninety degree turn at night. The road was narrow and had deep drainage ditches on both sides to catch the water run-off during the rainy season. One of the two soldiers aboard the LARC was pinned under the wheel hub of the LARC, which lay on its side. The other soldier, who was unhurt, called in to dispatch, using the radio. My good friend Charlie Lawton, who by now had been promoted to sergeant, came up to the nearby Company area and drove my jeep down to the accident site. The jeeps didn't have locking ignition switches but, instead had a length of chain welded to the floor, passed through the steering wheel and padlocked. He was able to drive the jeep moving only straight, with little steerage. He found the unhurt soldier furiously trying to dig his buddy out from under the LARC's wheel hub, using just his hands. I think Charlie wanted to use the jeep to transport the soldier once freed from under the wheel.

A wrecker came down to get the LARC off the soldier and back onto its wheels. An ambulance had been called and the soldier was taken to the US Air Force medical facility on the base. A portable X-Ray machine was swung over his chest. A doctor who seemed to be in charge examined the soldier, swung the X-Ray machine away and he was pronounced dead. We had a memorial service for him and I soon learned he was from Ozone Park in Queens, New York.

We came close to having another fatality that would actually have been a murder. One of our second platoon soldiers named Swan had gone into the NCO tent carrying his entrenching tool in an attempt to kill Sergeant Raynor. The other NCOs in the tent were able to subdue him. Entrenching tools are small, folding, shovel and pick combinations carried by soldiers to dig foxholes. It is quite heavy and could easily kill someone. I don't believe any MPs were called in. Instead, Lieutenant Doran set up a table and some chairs in the mess hall and had second platoon soldiers come in, one at a time, to be interviewed, regarding how people were being treated by

Sergeant Raynor. He found that Sergeant Raynor was often unnecessarily strict and uncaring about the people in his charge. Lieutenant Doran got about half way through the platoon when he stopped, having heard enough. He must have done something with the sergeant because he was better for about a month before resorting back to his old self.

I don't remember anything official taking place and no disciplinary action being taken with Swan. Maybe they took away his entrenching tool. Anyway, he later went on a pass to Pataya, which is a resort area, and where you could rent motorcycles. He had a bad accident with one of those motorcycles and was sent to a large military hospital in Japan. We heard he might not be able to walk again.

People think of the Army as being very strict and disciplined. While that is true during training "state side" and being on posts around the world, it was not so much in the bush. There was a definite kind of boys-will-be-boy's attitude much of the time. With Swan I saw how problems tended to be kept at the company level rather than reported to higher authority. I don't think these kinds of incidents bode well for the officers and NCO's abilities in leadership; too many problems would damage chances for promotion.

Bates again dodged a bullet when the driver taking over his LARC during a shift change found a pack of Marlboro cigarettes on the dashboard; the tobacco was emptied out and replaced with marijuana. The driver turned it in, thinking he didn't want to be found with it. Bates was called down to the Provost Marshall. I drove him there in my jeep. He went in for a while and came out unscathed and, worse, he wasn't leaving the 165th.

In yet another episode he was drunk or high on weed or both and he was horsing around with a tent mate called "Pineapple" since he was from Hawaii. Bates had him around the waist, swung him around, and Pineapple hit his head on the iron side rail of a bunk, he was bleeding profusely. Bates came running to me to get the jeep and drive him and Pineapple to the dispensary on the Air Force Base. When I brought the jeep around to his tent a couple of guys carried him to the back seat. I couldn't see the wound because there was a bloody towel wrapped around his head. I put the flashers on and braved the Air Force Police, speeding to the dispensary. Once we got to the dispensary Bates ran inside and got some medical personnel to help get Pineapple in.

In the back seat of the jeep I saw blood and some kind of matter. I thought it was brain matter. I waited with the jeep for a while wondering what could they possibly do for a guy whose brains were spilling out? Finally, I decided to go inside and see what was happening. To my surprise they had Pineapple on the treatment table, very much alive, and they had shaved the hair from around a one-inch gash in his scalp. Pineapple was not cooperating. Being drunk, he kept moving around while the doctor was trying to stitch the gash. Bates was holding him down as best he could and started to get weak knees, like he was going to faint. I tried to hold him and Pineapple. I told Bates not to faint with all of these glass cabinets all around us. There were even large glass jars full of alcohol or some kind of preservative containing different kinds of snakes. The idea was if you were bitten by a snake, and made it to the dispensary, you could identify the one that bit you.

Once Pineapple was patched up I went out to the jeep to see what was on the back seat. It turned out to be vomit.

Good thing I'm not a doctor.

I made many runs to the dispensary since the jeep was the handiest and fastest vehicle we had in the Company. Thankfully, the injuries were usually minor. For example: We had a LARC driver on night shift whose LARC was overheating. He went to the water tower we had just for that kind of event. The procedure was to get up on the walkway that went around the engine compartment where there were non-slip pads to walk on. You would place your boot on the radiator cap from a standing position, and twist it just enough to let the hissing and boiling water out. Once the geyser quieted down you could safely remove the cap and put water in from the hose that was fed from the water tower. The driver did not do this; rather, he just bent down and unscrewed the cap, looking directly at it. He got a face full of boiling water. With his eyes shut tight he climbed down from the LARC and went around yelling, "My eyes, my eyes."

I was summoned; I climbed out of my bunk, dressed and drove the guy to the dispensary. Luckily, he had not done any permanent damage to his eyes. He was given some kind of cream to use for the burn and sent back to the Company.

I loved being the second platoon jeep driver. The jeep with its white stars painted on the hood and sides was kind of an iconic vehicle for the US Army. It was fun to drive and was much easier to maintain than a LARC. Officers were not allowed to drive in Thailand. I asked Lieutenant Stone why that was. He told me, "If an officer was to get into a fatal accident with a Thai national it would be an international incident." Apparently, if it was an enlisted man, he would get hung out to dry. Nice. I would stay ready to drive Lieutenant Stone at any time. If he didn't have any place to go I would stay in the Orderly Room with First Sergeant Whitefield and the two Company clerks. The clerks knew everything that was going on so I heard all the news.

Lieutenants Stone and Masters came to my tent one day when we were off duty waiting for a ship to arrive. They asked, "Would you drive us to Pattaya?" Of course, I pulled my boots and fatigues on, got my jeep, and picked up the two officers at the Orderly Room. The drive to Pattaya was about forty-five minutes. Driving in Thailand was dangerous. The American vehicles had the steering wheel on the left as we are used to. This places the driver on the left shoulder of the road so if you had to pass a slow vehicle, of which there were many, you couldn't see to pass. If you had a passenger he could look down the middle of the road and let you know if it was safe. Thai drivers would constantly pass on hills and, while passing and coming at you head-on, would just flick their lights instead of moving back into their lane.

Our own Captain Posner was on his way in a jeep to headquarters with himself, two lieutenants and the driver when I got a call from First Sergeant Whitefield. He said over the radio that the Captain's jeep had been in an accident and he asked me to find him to see if I might be of help. I found the Captain on the road to Camp Vayama. The jeep was twelve feet off the road, lying upside down. All of the jeep's occupants were walking around and seemed unhurt. Army jeeps had no roll bars so turning over could be disastrous. In this instance the jeep's windshield and heavy antenna bracket at the rear of the jeep served the purpose. I then drove the Captain and the other two officers to headquarters while the driver stayed with the jeep, waiting for a wrecker to arrive.

I was asked by First Sergeant Whitefield to go to the local village to buy some fresh onions and, I think, garlic. One of our sergeants had taken up residence in the village so I followed him on my first trip. Now this was an interesting place. All the men and women wore sarongs but no tops. The men all carried machetes because they were tapioca farmers and used them to harvest the crop. The local kids who were in our Company area daily selling sodas to the GIs came from this village. Since I now knew how to get there I would go whenever the sergeants needed more fresh produce. I didn't speak much Thai and the inhabitants spoke no English. I would just point to what I wanted at the vegetable stand and they would look at the handful of money I offered, taking what they deemed a fair price. The money in Thailand was the baht and each baht was five cents U.S. They usually charged me five baht.

The kids we knew were beaming and showing off, climbing into the jeep. They were real proud that they knew the GIs; that's what they called us incessantly, "GI, Hey GI." At one point the jeep's radio went off with some chatter and they were startled. The adults kept their eyes on us but did not display any concern that we came into their village. On one of my trips I stopped by Joe Callahan's tent and asked him if he would like to take a ride. He jumped in and we took off. While we were in the village the kids became curious about us having hair on our arms and faces. They liked to pull on the hair and they called us *docling*. Some troops thought they were trying to say darling but we learned it meant monkey!

As we were driving back to our quarters we came upon a water buffalo wallowing in a small pond. We stopped because Joe wanted to get a picture of it. He got out of the jeep and went to the edge of the pond. The buffalo snorted and rose up from the water. It started moving toward the bank and Joe backed up. I kept the jeep in gear, with the clutch in, ready to take off. And take off we did. Looking back, we could see the buffalo had come right up to the road. I still have a picture of that.

We wondered why small children carrying little sticks could lead the water buffalos around and plow fields with them when we couldn't get near one without it making some aggressive moves. One idea was that we smelled different than the Thai people tending them.

We had a mail clerk, whom, I never liked. He had posted hours for mail call, and if someone was late it was, "sorry 'bout that," even if he was ten feet from the mail room. At times mail call would be over and someone would come down to the Orderly Room to see if he had any mail. He would be told, "No, you don't." The soldier would argue, "How do you know if you don't look?" The response would be, "because I sorted the mail and didn't see any for you."

I always suspected that he really didn't know; he just wouldn't get off his ass to check, and, worse, may have known that the guy did have mail. He finally left, his tour being over, and First

Sergeant Whitefield asked me to add mail clerk to my regular duties. I had to be interviewed and approved, I was given a card authorizing me to handle the U.S. Mail. It was a simple enough job, especially because I drove to headquarters each day anyway to deliver reports. The Morning Report had to be in each morning without fail. I picked up the basket with the incoming mail and turned in the outgoing mail. There were no stamps or fee required since we all got free mail service. In the tiny mail room there was one of those pigeonhole shelves with alpha letters on each box where you sorted the mail.

We still had regular mail call hours, but if anyone missed it and came to me I opened the mail room, even if they were very late and came down to my tent to find me. I knew how important mail was to the guys and wasn't going to deny them some news from loved ones.

First Sergeant Whitefield was a great NCO, he looked like General MacArthur. Air Force officers would come out to our Company area from time to time to look at the LARCs and get a ride on one. We thought this was funny since they were fighter pilots who probably experienced many more thrills than a LARC ride would provide. But they took pictures and loved it. They would drive up to the Orderly Room in their blue jeeps and we would let Sergeant Whitefield know they were approaching. As they entered the Orderly Room Sergeant Whitefield would loudly call "Atten-hut," which is the correct protocol for when an officer enters a room. We would all snap to attention' sometimes, with our chairs falling over. Not being as military as the Army, the Air Force officers would be taken aback, not knowing what they should do. They would ask "How do I get them back to what they were doing?" Someone would reply, "the order is, as you were, sir."

We were right near the Royal Thai Air Force Base and used some of their facilities. We regularly visited the EM club, the Base Exchange (BX) and the medical dispensary. In my travels I would take different routes at times to learn my way around. On one of those trips I found a vehicle car wash on the Air Force Base. It had four high pressure steam wands. The people operating this facility were all Thais and had no complaint about a US Army soldier using the steam cleaner. I was able to keep the jeep really clean, including the engine compartment. I never told the other three jeep drivers in my Company about the car wash. Not to have an advantage over them, but I figured if we overdid it someone from the Air Force would notice and we would be restricted from using it.

I had a flat tire and I changed it with the spare. I had noticed the Air Force guys had a vehicle maintenance area and they had one of those tire breaking machines. We didn't have a tire breaker but improvised by driving a truck over the wheel with the flat to break the tire and then used tire irons to get the tire off the rim. This was kind of haphazard and a lot of work. So I took my jeep over to the maintenance area I had found and asked the Thai guys working there to fix the flat. They readily agreed and got a brand new inner tube out to put in the tire. I tried to explain to them that I didn't need the inner tube; they could just patch the one I had. I was trying not to use the Air Force's material. They insisted on putting in the new tube and went on with the repair.

Just then an Air Force sergeant, with lots of stripes, came by and saw what was going on. He told me he would allow the mechanics to complete the tire repair but he wanted me to replace the tube with one from the Army's maintenance supplies. I said, "Yes, sergeant," and left as soon as the tire was mounted.

I went right down to the motor pool in my operations area and explained to my maintenance buddies that I needed a new inner tube to replace the one the Air Force had given me. They handed me the tube still in its plastic wrapper and I drove right back to the Air Force maintenance section. I met the sergeant there and gave him the new tube. He seemed surprised that I would return with the tube at all, let alone within an hour's time. I sensed that he liked this Army kid and he told me I could use his shop anytime I needed anything.

Sometime later we had a colonel come by to do an inspection of our vehicles. We were all told to stay in our quarters while the inspection was going on and would be called if needed. A runner came to my tent asking for me and telling me "Tuffy" wanted to see me, on the double. I ran down to where Tuffy, Captain Posner and the colonel were gathered near the parked jeeps. The Colonel pointed out my jeep and asked if it was assigned to me. I said, "Yes, sir", thinking I must be in some kind of trouble. Instead, the Colonel congratulated me on having a finely maintained vehicle and told me he had asked Captain Posner to place a commendation in my personnel file. Captain Posner and Warrant Officer "Tuffy" were beaming.

I made some points that day, thanks to the Air Force.

I liked being a soldier to the point where I was "spit and polish" as much as I could be, given the living conditions we had. At one time, the First Sergeant asked me to deliver a manila envelope to the Battalion Commander, Colonel Haverness. I was told not to give it to anyone in Headquarters except to the Colonel himself. I drove to Camp Vayama and found the Headquarters building. I entered and asked one of the clerks where I could find the Colonel.

They pointed me to a soldier sitting at a desk saying, "He's the Colonel's clerk." I went to him and asked to see the Colonel. He asked me why and I told him I had an envelope to deliver to him.

The clerk said, "Give it to me and I'll see that the Colonel gets it."

I said, "No, my orders are to give it to no one but the Colonel himself." He said, "I'm the Colonel's clerk and handle all of his correspondence."

I still refused. He started to get up to go into the Colonel's office and gave me a you're gonna' be in trouble look. He was only gone for a minute or two when he returned and told me to go in. I went in, stood at attention, in front of the Colonel's desk and identified myself and my purpose. The Colonel ordered me, "at ease" and took the envelope.

He then asked me about the 165th's touch football team who were winning every game they played. He asked me what I attributed this to. I told him, "I believe it's because we came overseas as a unit rather than as piecemeal replacements scattered everywhere, and as a result worked together really well." He found that interesting.

When I got back to my Company area and came into the Orderly Room, First Sergeant Whitefield told me that the Colonel had called to commend the soldier that had delivered the envelope and who was a fine representative of the 165th. He told Sergeant Whitefield that his driver was going home soon and what did he think of having SP/4 Capainolo take his place? First Sergeant Whitefield told the Colonel that I had only a few weeks left before I was to go home and that would leave the Colonel searching again for a new driver. The Colonel agreed.

The 165th football team went on to be the All Thailand Champions, beating Army, Marines, Air Force and Navy. Of course, Captain Posner was ecstatic.

Captain Posner was a good commanding officer (CO) but a lot of guys would say he was "bucking for Major.'' I'm sure he was, and why not? He was a career officer and had six kids. Some of the troops under his command would complain that we always had to put our best foot forward and work a little harder so he would look good. He did things like naming us the "Dolphin" Company and had likenesses of Dolphins everywhere you looked. Each tent had a little sign outside of it with the tent number painted in white over a rendering of a blue dolphin. There was a large wooden cut-out dolphin over the chow line in the mess hall.

One sour note was that his family had sent him a stuffed toy dolphin from the TV show "Flipper." When we were packing up everything for our transfer to Thailand some son of a bitch had gotten hold of the dolphin and slit it open, dumping out the stuffing and hanging the "carcass" on a light pole for all to see. I never got wind of who might have done it, but he was a poor excuse for a US Army soldier.

The soldier who did all of the sign painting for us was a guy named John Horan. At that time my young brother Peter, was in grammar school in Patchogue, Long Island, New York. My mother had asked me to send home some uniform patches so she could make a little soldier shirt for him. She made the shirt and he went to school wearing it. His young female teacher saw the shirt and asked him about it. He told her his brother was in the Army in Thailand. She told him that her friend's boyfriend was in the Army and was in Thailand, too. She wrote down his name and asked my mother to send it along on the off chance that I knew him. Well, I did in fact know him; he was the guy who was our sign painter. We took a picture of the both of us together and sent it to his girlfriend.

Chapter 18

The girls. Most people are aware that wherever there are troops posted there will be bars, sex shows and prostitutes nearby. Vietnam and Thailand were no exceptions. The strip, as it was called, had a mile or two row of bars. Prostitutes were readily available and they had plenty of customers. The problem was what we used to call VD (now STDs) was widespread. Each morning we had a truck with ten or fifteen soldiers being taken down to the dispensary to get their daily shot of penicillin to cure whatever it was they were suffering from. Thailand was a little better than Vietnam because the girls were required to be checked out for VD each week by the Thai government's medical people. They all had a little book about the size of a passport that was stamped with the results of the tests. The problem is they could always get infected by the very next client.

I was not inclined to avail myself of any of their services, especially since I am allergic to penicillin. One night at the Air Man's Club I saw a group of medics sitting at a table having some beers. I went over to them and asked what would happen if you contracted VD and were allergic to penicillin? They looked at each other and one of them said, "Know any good prayers?"

I said, "What about antibiotics?"

They told me, "There are strains of disease found in Thailand not seen in the U.S. and as a result the antibiotics don't work well." They went on to say, "If you get one of these diseases you are not allowed back to the U.S. until cured. When that would be was anyone's guess." It seemed appropriate that the Vietnamese band was playing a song they had written with the chorus being, "GI say sorry 'bout that, sorry 'bout that."

Good luck.

Besides bar girls, there were those who were not prostitutes and didn't visit any of the bars. A few guys dated the local indigenous personnel (LIPs) and some shared off-base living quarters with them. The first time I went to the Army EM club at camp Vayama I couldn't help but notice a beautiful waitress whom the troops called "Lucky." She was not only very pretty but had a very warm and friendly disposition. She was everyone's sweetheart but didn't date anyone, although she had many offers.

There came one exception, a soldier named Dale Holland who came from North Carolina. He looked like and became known as Rock, after the actor. He started dating Lucky regularly, and had her introduce Charlie Lawton to a friend of hers and they often double dated. They started staying out all night, making it back to the Company area just before morning formation.

This went on for a few months, and it was obvious that Holland had really fallen in love with this beautiful little Siamese doll and she with him. Not so with Charlie; he was just out for the dating fun and the girl knew it but enjoyed his company. One big problem; Holland was married to a girl back in North Carolina. The dilemma was that we were getting what the troops call "short," meaning we had only a hundred or less days left before heading back to the States. I remember there was heartbreak for the both of them, but I don't remember what, if anything was resolved. There was another soldier who had a place off base with his girlfriend. The word was that she had hung herself because he was leaving. I didn't really believe it at first, not until I saw the guy at the hotel in Bangkok where we stayed waiting for a flight back to the "world," as we called the U.S.A. You could see he was in pain. This is why a lot of girls asked out by soldiers didn't do so saying, "GIs same-same butterfly." Meaning they flitted from one girl to another.

My troubles with Bates continued. One night while I was asleep I awoke feeling a presence. I looked to the screen at the side of my bunk and saw Bates staring at me from four inches outside and saying, "Isn't it nice to be alive? Aren't you lucky to be alive?" He just made some crazy laughing sound, "Hyeesh" and went away.

Bates had gotten a machete, probably bought in Sattahip. He cut up his entire tent, making it look like strips of canvas. Here again, nothing was done about it. The tent was replaced with another and life with Bates went on.

One day while I was dressing in my tent a Thai guy came in, saying hello, and looking around acting kind of weird. He seemed to be high on something. He saw my watch on one of the two by fours framing the tent and grabbed it. I collared him, peeled his fingers off the watch and threw him through the tent door. Lucky for him, the door swung to the outside and he wasn't hurt. A few minutes later I heard a commotion outside and saw a couple of soldiers holding the guy and walking him down to the Orderly Room. Apparently, he went into someone's tent and stole a carton of cigarettes. First Sergeant Whitefield called the Air Police who came and put the guy in their jeep. They asked First Sergeant Whitefield to follow them to the Thai police station. First Sergeant Whitefield asked me to drive him. We followed the Air Police for about forty-five minutes. At one point they stopped for a bit so we pulled over as well. As we were waiting First Sergeant Whitefield asked me about Bates and why did the guys like him? Thinking he was great fun? I sensed he had heard about the tent getting cut up. I told the First Sergeant, "Only a few guys think he is fun; everyone else is wary of him." Again, no action taken.

Sitting there in the jeep with First Sergeant Whitefield, we got into a discussion. We had recently received six replacements who were infantry and they all were wearing their Combat Infantry

Badges (CIBs). Only infantrymen who had been in combat for a minimum of seventy-two hours were given this award. I told First Sergeant Whitefield that I didn't feel as much a soldier as these guys. I said I was in the Army, doing work supporting combat operations by delivering the means to destroy the enemy, but not actually engaging the enemy. Sergeant Whitefield told me that support units such as the 165[th.] have been in many combat situations. He told me I was every bit a soldier as them; coming from him, that meant a lot to me.

The Thai police station looked like a very bad place. There was a deck about eight feet above the ground held up by poles where the office was. The area below the deck was fenced in with prisoners, shoulder to shoulder, standing on the dirt floor. I began to feel sorry for the guy who stole the carton of cigarettes.

On another psychotic occasion Bates had taken a bail of string and completely strung it all around his tent so that it looked like a giant spider web. The guys assigned to the tent had to cut their way through to get to their bunks. After the "Aren't you lucky to be alive" incident, I bought myself a combat knife like the kind the Marines call a "K-Bar" and slept with it under my pillow. I had only eighteen days left before going back to the States, and I prayed nothing would happen. I knew if there was any kind of fight with weapons I certainly would face a long investigation, delaying any  chance of getting home on schedule. A bad deal, but better than dead.

Bates came into my tent one night while I was lying on my bunk; all my tent mates were on night shift, so I was alone. Bates barged into my tent breathing heavily and making noises like some kind of rampaging animal. I slipped my hand under my pillow and gripped the knife handle tightly. Our tents were the standard eight-man version. Bates came in the back door and went to the first bunk on his right feeling the bunk, looking for me. I was not in that bunk but in the one straight across the aisle from the one he had searched. Inexplicably, instead of crossing the center aisle, he went diagonally across and missed me. All I could think about was the machete he used to cut up the tent, and did he have it with him now? I can't say because it was so dark. By the grace of God, he missed me entirely and left.

You can bet I didn't sleep that night and not much for the next eighteen nights either.

Who needed the Vietcong to worry about when you had Bates?

Chapter 19

Preparations were being made for the 165th to have a beer party in our mess hall with Thai girls in bikinis as waitresses. First Sergeant Whitefield was in charge of hiring the girls and I drove him down the "strip," stopping at various bars.

One of the larger and better known bars was called "The Sweet Dreams," and we stopped there. While we were outside the bar sitting in my jeep the Captain, whose call sign on the radio was 6, called for First Sergeant Whitefield who was 6 Alpha. I was designated as 2 Delta. The radio transmission heard by the entire Company on their radios was, "6 Alpha this is 6."

6 Alpha responded with, "6 this is 6 Alpha."

The Captain came back with, "6 Alpha, this is 6, what is your ETA for Company CP?' (Command Post).

"6 this is 6 Alpha, we'll be heading back as soon as I can get 2 Delta out of the "Sweet Dreams."

Everyone had a good laugh, including the Captain.

The bikini clad waitresses weren't *exactly* waitresses and some were solicited for other activities. One did a strip show, planned, not impromptu. I thought some guys, particularly the married ones, were taking a big chance so close to leaving risking disease and taking home an unwanted package.

Pretty soon the 165th was abuzz with activity as preparations were made to rotate out and head back to "the world." Before leaving for Vietnam we had all been told to send our dress green uniforms home since it was not the dress uniform worn in Southeast Asia. The dress uniform for this warm climate was khakis. We had our people at home send the "greens" to us since they would be worn when we got to California. Most of us had changes to be made, like sewing on unit patches and insignias of rank. There was a tailor and dry cleaning establishment on the Air Force Base and we got our uniforms in order. There was some trading going on for people who had lost or gained weight. My uniform was tight on me so I traded with a guy who had lost weight. We both had good fits.

We shined our brass insignia and belt buckles with Brasso. We packed our duffle bags, made sure we had copies of our orders, and said goodbyes to friends. We climbed onto the "deuce and a half" that would take us to Bangkok. It was a dream come true, and no Bates. He was in a separate group; good riddance. On arrival at Bangkok, we found ourselves again at the Fortuna Hotel. I shared a room with Joe Callahan. Typical of the Army, as we all knew, was "hurry up and wait." So we spent three days at the Fortuna, enjoying air conditioning, a swimming pool, room service and all the amenities, it was like being on vacation.

I had gone up to my room and was shaving when Joe Callahan came in and told me that First Sergeant Whitefield had been asking for me. He had just gone to the airport to catch an earlier flight home because he had gotten word that his mother was very sick. I always regretted not saying goodbye to him. He was a man you would always remember, whether or not you liked the Army.

We got to the airport, and while seated in the terminal I heard over the PA; "MAC (Military Assistance Command) flight 60, will be boarding for departure from Bangkok to Tokyo, Japan for refueling and on to Travis Air Force Base, California."

At that moment, hearing that announcement, I really felt I was going home.

Once boarded I again was with Joe Callahan. We had been together since basic training. Since so much of the time assignments were handed out in alphabetical order and Joe's first three letters being "Call," and mine "Cap," meant we were usually together. On this flight Joe was seated on the aisle. I sat in the middle, next to an Air Force Colonel on my left at the window seat. What do you talk about with a Colonel? He actually made us feel very relaxed and was kind of a grandfatherly guy. The first leg of our trip was six hours. When we landed in Tokyo for a refueling stop we got off the plane and found that it was cold. All we had on was our short sleeved cotton Khakis. After refueling we took off for an eleven-hour flight to Travis Air Force Base in California.

At Travis we were greeted by a PFC holding a clip board with all of our names on it. He called out names for a head count and we were all present. I marvel at the Army's record keeping in the days before computers, and word processors, with everything required in multiple copies. Curiously, the Army paperwork, with its thousands of abbreviations did not use periods following abbreviations. In the Orderly Room I often helped out when it was discovered that I could type. I had to get used to not using periods after abbreviations. If you inadvertently used one, the entire report had to be corrected. It took some getting used to.

The customs check was just a cursory look into the top of our duffel bags, and then we boarded the bus that would take us to Oakland Army Terminal. It was great looking at cars in the parking lot: Fords, Chevys, Dodges, etc. There was a bus waiting to take us to the terminal. Once there we changed into our dress green uniforms. Because we arrived late in the day we would not complete the separation process until the next day. There were bunks for us to use but we didn't get much sleep, anxious to become civilians again. As we made our way the next morning to the various clerical stations we ran into Lieutenants Doran and Masters. I was glad we had the chance to say goodbye and wish them well. They were really good officers. The last stop was at a table with cardboard boxes full of large envelopes bearing the seal of the Department of Defense with a Lieutenant who asked our names and found our envelopes. Looking at my address on the envelope the Lieutenant joked, "Do you really want to go back to Patchogue, New York?"

I answered, "yes sir."

He handed me my envelope.

Separation papers and travel expense money in hand, Joe Callahan and I shared a taxi to San Francisco Airport. Joe was headed back to his home in Youngstown, Ohio and I was headed for Patchogue, Long Island. We shook hands, wished each other well and headed to our respective boarding areas. It was about a five-hour flight to JFK, and after flying seventeen hours from Bangkok to California I was pretty sick of sitting on an airplane. The plane had few passengers. The stewardess, or flight attendant, in today's parlance was very nice and wondered why I didn't want any dinner. I told her, "I'm not air sick; I just have had enough of airplane food."

It was a pleasant flight and we landed at JFK in the early morning hours. I wanted to go to Penn. Station to get a train to Patchogue but there were no cabs at the cab stand at this hour. I just waited, looking out the window for any cabs. Standing nearby in the empty terminal was a young Army private and his parents. I was aware of them looking at me and I could guess what was going to happen next. The father came up to me and said that his son could tell by my award ribbons and combat patch that I had been in Vietnam. He said, "My wife is very upset, do you think you could speak with her and assure that our son would be O.K.?"

What could I say? I went with the father back to his wife and son and knew the soldier was probably dying of embarrassment. So I tried to make it brief. I told them, "It isn't like the TV news, showing combat all of the time." I said, "there is an old saying that a soldier's life is ninety-nine percent boredom interrupted by one percent terror." I wished him, "Good luck," shook his hand and went back to watching for a taxi.

I finally got a taxi that took me to Penn. Station. After exiting the taxi, I started down the steps and became immediately aware of the grime and trash on the steps. The light, clean airport at San Francisco came to my mind. Everywhere I looked at Penn. Station I saw grunge and gritty-looking people. At the ticket booth there was a drunk buying a ticket, along with a blonde woman I took to be his girlfriend. I said to myself, *"The train will be almost empty and I'll probably end up with this drunk in my car."*

Sure enough, the drunk and the woman were in the same car with me. The guy kept looking at me and started in with, "Hey, soldier boy." I just ignored him and pretty soon the conductor spoke with him and he went on to something else. A few stops later he got off but the woman stayed on, speaking with the conductor. It occurred to me that she was a prostitute who was now between engagements, with the conductor potentially the next customer.

Welcome home to New York, "Soldier Boy."

Acknowledgments

My wife, Julia, served on the committee that built the Vietnam Veterans Memorial from its inception to its final construction. It's a beautiful piece of architecture, standing upon Bald Hill, in Farmingville, New York, one of the highest points on Long Island. It is located on Patchogue-Mount Sinai Road, Suffolk County Rt. 83.

It was officially dedicated on Veterans' Day, November 11, 1991.

Julia performed a major part in proof reading and helped make the book as error free as we could make possible.

Vietnam Veterans Memorial, Farmingville, NY

Joe Callahan, my friend ever since we went through Basic Combat Training at Fort Jackson, SC. He supplied most of the photographs and helped with identifying people whose names had escaped me.

Eileen Obser, editor, author and teacher at my memoir writing group held at the Connetquot Public library, in Bohemia, NY. Eileen gave me much encouragement to write the book.

My Brother Peter, who did an excellent job of proof reading the work.

Bob Lee, one of my oldest friends, and a longtime colleague while we worked at a communications company. He was my guitar teacher, and someone who encouraged me and put up with my constant jabbering about the book writing.

USARSUPTHAI an organization dedicated to those who served in Vietnam and Thailand. And particularly Joseph J. Wilson Jr .and Joseph Murphy, both of whom provided valuable information.

Epilogue

After my time with the 165TH and having returned to my home, the 165th went on to distinguish themselves in combat just as First Sergeant Whitefield had advised me that Transportation Corps. troops did indeed serve in combat when called upon.

Printed herein, courtesy of, and with the permission of, a veterans' organization known as USARSUPTHAU. Visit their website for more information:

On 18 March 1968, personnel from the 165th Transportation Company (Light Amphibian) combined with personnel from the 347th Transportation Company (Light Amphibian) sailed from Thailand and arrived at Thon My Thuy, Vietnam on 2 Mar 1968 and joined the remainder of the unit assigned to the 159th Transportation Battalion (Terminal) known as "Sunders Wonders" provided command and control for the LOTS (Logistics Over the Shore) operation at Wunder Beach" and was the most significant LOTS operations ever conducted during the Vietnam War.

The beaches all along I Corps had too shallow a gradient for landing craft to drop ramp on dry shore. Therefore, only amphibious vehicles from the 165th Transportation Company (Amphibious Light) and Provisional BARC Companies could conduct the ship-to-shore lighterage.

Immediately upon arrival in country Vietnam, the personnel of the unit were faced with precarious task of forging a base of operations

160

on an isolated beach deep within hostile territory. Although subjected to constant enemy harassment, they worked on a twenty-four-hour basis to establish a defensive perimeter and adequate living and working conditions in the remarkably short period of four days. The LOTS operation supported the 1st Cavalry Division during Operations PEGAUS and DELAWARE to break the siege of Khe Sanh and drive the NVA out of the A Shau Valley although the 165th Transportation Company (Light Amphibian) and their fleet of 25 LARCs were subjected to constant attacks from enemy fire.

The LOTS operation at Wunder Beach, near Quang Tri, fortunately provided MACV with the additional tonnage needed to conduct its counter-offensive to relieve Khe Sanh and drive the NVA out of I Corps Zone. This was only possible due to the skill and efficiency with which men at Wunder Beach moved cargo from ship-to-shore and inland. A typhoon closed down the operation in September. Thus, they far exceeded the expectations of MACV skeptics and delivered the means for victory.

Realizing the importance of civic actions to the ultimate success of the war effort, the men of the company organized a vigorous assistance and transportation program to replenish vitally needed food supplies for the isolated island of Bai Lue. The 165th Transportation Company (Light Amphibian) and 253rd Transportation Company (Amphibious Maintenance Direct Support) were awarded the Meritorious Unit Commendation on 3 May 1969 for their work at Wunder Beach during the period 21 March 1968 to 26 September 1968.

On 19 October 1968 an urgent call came in to assist B Company, 87th Engineer Battalion in the evacuation of their campsite that became stranded by high waters.

The crews of two amphibious LARC's were dispatched south of Cam Ranh Bay on QL-1 highway and successfully completed their mission and were recognized by a Letter of Appreciation from the Battalion Commander of the 87th Engineer Battalion.

Those recognized were SSG Nathaniel Issard, SP4 Raymond M. Cox, SP4 William Robertson, SP4 Murry Konev's, PFC William F. Coffey, PFC Paul K. Combs, PFC Ronald Hall, and PVT Leendert Dan Brave.

The 165th Transportation Company (Light Amphibian) was inactivated in Thailand on 1 November 1968. The company continued to operate until all personnel had become reassigned on 22 Jan 1969.

DEPARTMENT OF THE ARMY
Lineage and Honors
165TH TRANSPORTATION DETACHMENT

Constituted 3 November 1944 in the Army of the United States as the 3363d Quartermaster Service Detachment

Activated 12 December 1944 in the Philippines

Reorganized and predesignated 1 April 1945 as the 3363d Quartermaster Driver Detachment

Inactivated 24 September 1945 in the Philippines

Converted and redesignated 1 August 1946 as the 3363d Transportation Corps Driver Detachment

Redesignated 10 October 1961 as the 165th Transportation Detachment and allotted to the Regular Army

Activated 11 October 1961 in Germany

Inactivated 28 June 1963 in Germany

Activated 18 March 1965 at Fort Riley, Kansas

Inactivated 25 November 1968 in Vietnam

Assigned 1 September 1969 to the 1st Cavalry Division and activated in Vietnam

The Lighter Side of Vietnam

Inactivated 30 June 1971 in Vietnam and relieved from assignment to the 1st Cavalry Division

Activated 16 September 1979 in Germany

Inactivated 1 June 1993 in Germany

Activated 17 May 2009 at Fort Riley, Kansas

CAMPAIGN PARTICIPATION CREDIT

World War II
Luzon

Vietnam
Defense
Counteroffensive
Counteroffensive, Phase II
Counteroffensive, Phase III
Tet Counteroffensive
Counteroffensive, Phase IV
Counteroffensive, Phase V
Counteroffensive, Phase VI
Summer-Fall 1969
Winter-Spring 1970
Sanctuary Counteroffensive
Counteroffensive, Phase VII

War on Terrorism
Campaigns to be determined

DECORATIONS

Valorous Unit Award, Streamer embroidered PLEI ME

Meritorious Unit Commendation (Army), Streamer embroidered AFGHANISTAN 2010-2011

Philippine Presidential Unit Citation, Streamer embroidered 17 OCTOBER 1944 TO 4 JULY 1945

Republic of Vietnam Cross of Gallantry with Palm, Streamer embroidered VIETNAM 1966-1967

Republic of Vietnam Cross of Gallantry with Palm, Streamer embroidered VIETNAM 1967-1968

Republic of Vietnam Cross of Gallantry with Palm, Streamer embroidered VIETNAM 1969-1970

Republic of Vietnam Civil Action Honor Medal, First Class, Streamer embroidered VIETNAM 1969-1970

BY ORDER OF THE SECRETARY OF THE ARMY:

ROBERT   J.   DALESSANDRO
Director, Center of Military History

165thTransportation Company
Meritorious Unit Citation: 21 March 1968 – 26 September 1968 (DAGO 42, 1969)
Meritorious Unit Citation: 1 November 1968 – 29 August 1969 (DAGO 51, 1971)
Meritorious Unit Citation: 1 August 1971 – 30 April 1972 (DAGO 32, 1973)
Vietnamese Civic Action Unit Citation with Palm: 1 January 1971 – 31 December 1971 (DAGO 32, 1973)

Made in the USA
Columbia, SC
26 June 2018